MATH SKILLS FOR LAW ENFORCEMENT EXAMS

Other titles of interest from LearningExpress, LLC

Reasoning Skills for Law Enforcement Exams

MATH SKILLS FOR LAW ENFORCEMENT EXAMS

1st Edition

LEARNING EXPRESS ®

NEW YORK

Copyright © 2010 LearningExpress, LLC.

All rights reserved under International and Pan-American Copyright Conventions. Published in the United States by LearningExpress, LLC, New York.

Library of Congress Cataloging-in-Publication Data:
Math skills for law enforcement exams.—1st ed.
     p. cm.
  ISBN 978-1-57685-722-9
   1. Mathematics—Problems, exercises, etc.   2. Police—Vocational guidance—United States.
I. LearningExpress (Organization)
  QA43.M29825   2010
  510—dc22

                                          2009036630

Printed in the United States of America

9 8 7 6 5 4 3 2 1

First Edition

ISBN-10: 1-57685-722-0
ISBN-13: 978-1-57685-722-9

For information on LearningExpress, other LearningExpress products, or bulk sales, please write to us at:
  LearningExpress
  2 Rector Street
  26th Floor
  New York, NY 10006

Or visit us at:
  www.learnatest.com

CONTENTS

MATH SKILLS
FOR LAW
ENFORCEMENT
EXAMS

1 ▶ How to Use This Book

A career in law enforcement can be very rewarding. Whether you have just started, or have worked for several years, having strong math skills is important for success on the job. You may even have to take a test to be hired for some law enforcement jobs and math competency could be required. Maybe you haven't used your math skills in a while, or maybe you need to improve your math skills to move on to a better job, or simply to succeed at the job you are doing. Whatever the situation, by making the commitment to practice your math skills, you are promising yourself increased success and marketability. With over 200 on-the-job practice questions in arithmetic, word problems, measurement, basic geometry, and data analysis, this book is designed just for you.

About *Math Skills for Law Enforcement Exams*

You should carefully read this chapter and Chapter 2: The LearningExpress Test Preparation System so you can grasp effective strategies and learn to make the most of the chapters in this book. When you finish this chapter, take the 80-question diagnostic exam. Don't worry if you haven't studied math for a while. Your score on the diagnostic exam will help you gauge your current level of math skills and show you which lessons you need to review the most. After you take the diagnostic exam, you can refer to the answer explanations to see exactly how to solve each of the questions. The questions are meant to reflect the math skills tested on a variety of law enforcement exams, including:

- Corrections Officer Exam
- Federal Agent Exam
- Police Officer Exam
- State Police Exam
- Special Agent Exam
- Deputy Sheriff Exam

Before you take the diagnostic exam, let's review some basic math strategies.

Math Strategies

These suggestions are tried and true. You may use one or all of them. Or, you may decide to pick and choose the combination that works best for you.

- It is best not to work in your head! Use scratch paper to take notes, draw pictures, and calculate. Although you might think that you can solve math questions more quickly in your head, that's a good way to make mistakes. Instead, write out each step.

- Before you begin to make your calculations, read a math question in chunks rather than straight through from beginning to end. As you read each chunk, stop to think about what it means. Then make notes or draw a picture to represent that chunk.

- When you get to the actual question, circle it. This will keep you more focused as you solve the problem.

- Glance at the answer choices for clues. If they are fractions, you should do your work in fractions; if they are decimals, you should work in decimals, and so on.

- Develop a plan of attack to help you solve the problem. When you get your answer, reread the circled question to make sure you have answered it. This helps avoid the careless mistake of answering the wrong question.

- Always check your work after you get an answer. You may have a false sense of security when you get an answer that matches one of the multiple-choice answers. It could be right, but you should always check your work. Remember to:
  - Ask yourself if your answer is reasonable, if it makes sense.
  - Plug your answer back into the problem to make sure the problem holds together.
  - Do the question a second time, but use a different method.
  - Approximate when appropriate. For example:

$5.98 + $8.97 is a little less than $15. (Add: $6 + $9)

.9876 × 5.0342 is close to 5. (Multiply: 1 × 5)

- Skip questions that you find difficult and come back to them later. Make a note about them so you can find them quickly.

Review and Practice

Once you have completed the diagnostic exam and reviewed all the answer explanations, you are ready to move on to the review lessons and practice questions. When you have completed each chapter, you are ready to see how much you have improved. Chapters 12 and 13 include two 80-question practice exams covering the same types of math you will have studied in the previous chapters. Again, if you don't understand a question, the practice exams are followed by answer explanations to help you. When you are finished, compare your score on the diagnostic exam to your score on the practice exams and see how much you have improved!

Good luck!

2 ▶ The LearningExpress Test Preparation System

Taking any test can be tough, but don't let the written test scare you. If you prepare ahead of time, you can achieve a top score. The LearningExpress Test Preparation System, developed exclusively for LearningExpress by leading test experts, gives you the discipline and attitude you need to be a winner.

First, the bad news: Getting ready for any test takes work. If you plan to obtain a law enforcement position, you will have to score well on your relevant exam. This book focuses specifically on the math skills that you will be tested on—an area that has proven difficult for many test takers. By homing in on these skills, you will take your first step toward achieving the career of your dreams. However, there are all sorts of pitfalls that can prevent you from doing your best on exams. Here are some obstacles that can stand in the way of your success.

- being unfamiliar with the format of the exam
- being paralyzed by test anxiety
- leaving your preparation until the last minute
- not preparing at all

- not knowing vital test-taking skills like:
  - how to pace yourself through the exam
  - how to use the process of elimination
  - when to guess
- not being in tip-top mental and physical shape
- forgetting to eat breakfast and having to take the test on an empty stomach
- forgetting a sweater or jacket and shivering through the exam

What's the common denominator in all these test-taking pitfalls? One word: *control*. Who's in control, you or the exam?

Now the good news: The LearningExpress Test Preparation System puts *you* in control. In just nine easy-to-follow steps, you will learn everything you need to know to make sure you are in charge of your preparation and performance on the exam. *Other* test takers may let the test get the better of them; *other* test takers may be unprepared or out of shape, but not *you*. You will have taken all the steps you need to take for a passing score.

Here's how the LearningExpress Test Preparation System works: Nine easy steps lead you through everything you need to know and do to get ready to master your exam. The steps that follow give you tips and activities to help you prepare for any exam. It's important that you follow the advice and do the activities, or you won't be getting the full benefit of the system. First, here is a list of the steps with approximate time estimates.

Step 1. Get Information	30 minutes
Step 2. Conquer Test Anxiety	20 minutes
Step 3. Make a Plan	50 minutes
Step 4. Learn to Manage Your Time	10 minutes
Step 5. Learn to Use the Process of Elimination	20 minutes
Step 6. Know When to Guess	20 minutes
Step 7. Reach Your Peak Performance Zone	10 minutes
Step 8. Get Your Act Together	10 minutes
Step 9. Do It!	10 minutes
Total	3 hours

You estimate that working through the entire system will take you approximately three hours, though it's perfectly okay if you work faster or slower than the time estimates. If you can take a whole afternoon or evening, you can work through the entire LearningExpress Test Preparation System in one sitting. Otherwise, you can break it up, and do just one or two steps a day for the next several days. It's up to you—remember, *you're* in control.

Step 1: Get Information

Time to complete: 30 minutes
Activities: Read Chapter 1

If you haven't already done so, stop here and read Chapter 1. Here, you'll learn how to use this book.

Knowledge is power. The first step in the LearningExpress Test Preparation System is finding out everything you can about the types of questions that will be asked on any math section of your law enforcement exam. Practicing and studying the exercises in this book will help prepare you for those tests. Math topics that may be tested on your specific law enforcement test include:

- arithmetic
- powers
- fractions
- decimals
- ratios
- proportions
- percents
- word problems
- charts, tables, and graphs
- geometry
- measurement

After completing the LearningExpress Test Preparation System and the diagnostic exam (Chapter 3), you will then begin to apply the test-taking strategies you learn as you work through practice questions in the listed topic areas (Chapters 4 through 11). You can see how well your training paid off in Chapters 12 and 13, where you will take two practice exams based on all the topics covered in this book.

Step 2: Conquer Test Anxiety

Time to complete: 20 minutes
Activity: Take the Test Stress Test
Having complete information about the exam is the first step in getting control of the exam. Next, you have to overcome one of the biggest obstacles to test success: test anxiety. Test anxiety not only impairs your performance on the exam itself, but it can even keep you from preparing! In this step, you'll learn stress management techniques that will help you succeed on your exam. Learn these strategies now, and practice them as you work through the practice tests in this book, so they'll be second nature to you by exam day.

Combating Test Anxiety

The first thing you need to know is that a little test anxiety is a good thing. Everyone gets nervous before a big exam—and if that nervousness motivates you to prepare thoroughly, so much the better. It's said that Sir Laurence Olivier, one of the foremost British actors of the 20th century, was ill before every performance. His stage fright didn't impair his performance; in fact, it probably gave him a little extra edge—just the kind of edge you need to do well, whether on a stage or in an exam room.

On pages 8 and 9 is the Test Stress Test. Stop here and answer the questions on that page to find out whether your level of test anxiety is something you should worry about.

Stress Management before the Test

If you feel your level of anxiety getting the best of you in the weeks before the test, here is what you need to do to bring the level down again:

- **Get prepared.** There's nothing like knowing what to expect. Being prepared will put you in control of test anxiety. That's why you're reading this book. Use it faithfully, and remind yourself that you're better prepared than most of the people taking the test.
- **Practice self-confidence.** A positive attitude is a great way to combat test anxiety. This is no time to be humble or shy. Stand in front of the mirror and say to your reflection, "I'm prepared. I'm full of self-confidence. I'm going to ace this test. I know I can do it." Say it into a tape recorder and play it back once a day. If you hear it often enough, you'll believe it.
- **Fight negative messages.** Every time someone starts telling you how hard the exam is or that it's almost impossible to get a high score, start telling them your self-confidence messages above. If the someone with the negative messages is you, telling yourself you don't do well on exams and you just can't do this, don't listen. Turn on your tape recorder and listen to your self-confidence messages.
- **Visualize.** Imagine yourself reporting for your first day on the job. Visualizing success can help make it happen—and it helps you remember why you're preparing for the exam so diligently.
- **Exercise.** Physical activity helps calm down your body and focus your mind. Besides, being in good physical shape can actually help you do well on the exam. Go for a run, lift weights, go swimming—and do it regularly.

Stress Management on Test Day

There are several ways you can bring down your level of test anxiety on test day. To find a comfort level, experiment with the following exercises in the weeks before the test, and use the ones that work best for you.

- **Deep breathing.** Take a deep breath. Hold it while you count to five, then let it out. Repeat several times.
- **Move your body.** Try rolling your head in a circle. Rotate your shoulders. Shake your hands from the wrist. Many people find these movements very relaxing.
- **Visualize again.** Think of the place where you are most relaxed: lying on the beach in the sun, walking through the park, or sipping a cup of hot tea. Now close your eyes and imagine you're actually there. If you practice in advance, you'll find that you need only a few seconds of this exercise to experience a significant increase in your sense of well-being.

When anxiety threatens to overwhelm you right there during the exam, there are still things you can do to manage your stress level.

- **Repeat your self-confidence messages.** You should have them memorized by now. Say them quietly to yourself, and believe them!
- **Visualize one more time.** This time, visualize yourself moving smoothly and quickly through the test answering every question right and finishing just before time is up. Like most visualization techniques, this one works best if you've practiced it ahead of time.
- **Find an easy question.** Skim over the test until you find an easy question, and then answer it. Filling in even one circle gets you into the test-taking groove.

- **Take a mental break.** Everyone loses concentration once in a while during a long test. It's normal, so you shouldn't worry about it. Instead, accept what has happened. Say to yourself, "Hey, I lost it there for a minute. My brain is taking a break." Put down your pencil, close your eyes, and do some deep breathing for a few seconds. Then you're ready to go back to work.

Try these techniques ahead of time, and see if they work for you.

Test Stress Test

You only need to worry about test anxiety if it is extreme enough to impair your performance. The following questionnaire will provide a diagnosis of your level of test anxiety. In the blank before each statement, write the number that most accurately describes your experience.

0 = never
1 = once or twice
2 = sometimes
3 = often

_____ I have gotten so nervous before an exam that I simply put down the books and didn't study for it.

_____ I have experienced disabling physical symptoms such as vomiting and severe headaches because I was nervous about an exam.

_____ I have simply not showed up for an exam because I was scared to take it.

_____ I have experienced dizziness and disorientation while taking an exam.

_____ I have had trouble filling in the little circles because my hands were shaking too hard.

_____ I have failed an exam because I was too nervous to complete it.

_____ Total: Add up the numbers in the blanks above.

Your Test Stress Score

Here are the steps you should take, depending on your score. If you scored:

- **Below 3:** your level of test anxiety is nothing to worry about; it's probably just enough to give you the motivation to excel.
- **Between 3 and 6:** your test anxiety may be enough to impair your performance, and you should practice the stress management techniques listed in this section to try to bring your test anxiety down to manageable levels.
- **Above 6:** your level of test anxiety is a serious concern. In addition to practicing the stress management techniques listed in this section, you may want to seek additional, personal help. Call your local high school or community college and ask for the academic counselor. Tell the counselor that you have a level of test anxiety that sometimes keeps you from being able to take an exam. The counselor may be willing to help you or may suggest someone else you should talk to.

Step 3: Make a Plan

Time to complete: 50 minutes
Activity: Construct a study plan.
Maybe the most important thing you can do to get control of yourself and your exam is to make a study plan. Too many people fail to prepare simply because they fail to plan. Spending hours on the day before the exam poring over sample test questions not only raises your level of test anxiety, it is also no substitute for careful preparation and practice.

Don't fall into the cram trap. Take control of your preparation time by mapping out a study schedule. If you're the kind of person who needs deadlines and assignments to motivate you for a project, here they are. If you're the kind of person who doesn't like to follow other people's plans, you can use the suggested schedules here to construct your own.

Even more important than making a plan is making a commitment. You can't review everything you need to know for a law enforcement exam in one night. You have to set aside some time every day for study and practice. Try for at least 20 minutes a day. Twenty minutes daily will do you much more good than two hours on Saturday.

Don't put off your study until the day before the exam. Start now. A few minutes a day, with half an hour or more on weekends can make a big difference in your score.

If you have months before the exam, you're lucky. Don't put off your studying until the week before the exam. Start now. Even ten minutes a day, with half an hour or more on weekends, can make a big difference in your score—and in your chances of making the grade you want!

Schedule A: The 30-Day Plan

If you have at least one month before you take your test, you have plenty of time to prepare—as long as you don't procrastinate! If you have less than a month, turn to Schedule B.

Day 1: Skim over any written materials you may have about your specific law enforcement exam. Learn the specific content that you need to brush up on to prepare for the test. Read Chapter 1 of this book.

Day 2: Take the diagnostic exam and score yourself. Review any questions that you answered incorrectly. Make note of what chapters review the skills in these questions.

Days 3 and 4: Read Chapter 4 and practice these basic skills by working through the practice questions.

Day 5: Review any Chapter 4 concepts that you feel you need to brush up on.

Days 6 and 7: Read Chapter 5. Work through the practice questions and score yourself.

Day 8: Review any Chapter 5 concepts that you feel you need to brush up on.

Days 9 and 10: Read Chapter 6. Work through the practice questions. Score yourself.

Day 11: Review any Chapter 6 concepts you feel you need to brush up on.

Days 12 and 13: Read Chapter 7 and work through the practice questions. Score yourself.

Day 14: Review any Chapter 7 concepts that you feel you need to brush up on.

Days 15 and 16: Read Chapter 8 and work through the practice questions. Score yourself.

Day 17: Review any Chapter 8 concepts you feel you need to brush up on.

Days 18 and 19: Read Chapter 9 and work through the practice questions. Score yourself.

Day 20: Review any Chapter 9 concepts you feel you need to brush up on.

Days 21 and 22: Read Chapter 10 and work through the practice questions. Score yourself.

Day 23: Review any Chapter 10 concepts you feel you need to brush up on.

Days 24 and 25: Read Chapter 11 and work through the practice questions. Score yourself.

Day 26: Review any Chapter 11 concepts you feel you need to brush up on.

Day 27: In Chapter 12, take Practice Exam 1. Score yourself and review any questions you answered incorrectly. Review chapters covering skills that you might have missed on Practice Exam 1.

Day 28: In Chapter 13, take Practice Exam 2. Score yourself and review any questions you answered incorrectly. Then, review any concepts that you feel you need to brush up on. Work through similar questions in the appropriate chapters.

Day 29: Read through the Glossary of Math Terms. If you choose, make index cards for unfamiliar items. Review the chapters that contain the topics you were weak on during the Practice Exams.

Day before the Exam: Relax. Do something unrelated to the exam and go to bed at a reasonable hour.

Schedule B: The 14-Day Plan

If you have two weeks or less before the exam, you may have your work cut out for you. Use this 14-day schedule to help you make the most of your time.

Day 1: Read Chapter 1. Take the diagnostic exam in Chapter 3.

Day 2: Complete Chapter 4, including the practice questions.

Day 3: Complete Chapter 5, including the practice questions.

Day 4: Complete Chapter 6, including the practice questions.

Day 5: Complete Chapter 7, including the practice questions.

Day 6: Complete Chapter 8, including the practice questions.

Day 7: Complete Chapter 9, including the practice questions.

Day 8: Complete Chapter 10, including the practice questions.

Day 9: Complete Chapter 11, including the practice questions.

Day 10: Complete Practice Exam 1 (Chapter 12) and score yourself. Review all the questions that you missed.

Day 11: Review any concepts you feel you need to brush up on. Work through similar questions in the appropriate chapters. Study the appendix material.

Day 12: Complete Practice Exam 2 (Chapter 13) and score yourself. Review all the questions that you missed.

Day 13: Review any topics as indicated by the questions you missed on the practice tests. Then, look at the questions you missed again and make sure you understand them.

Day before the Exam: Relax. Do something unrelated to the exam and go to bed at a reasonable hour.

Step 4: Learn to Manage Your Time

Time to complete: 10 minutes to read, many hours of practice!

Activities: Use these strategies as you take the sample tests in this book.

Steps 4, 5, and 6 of the LearningExpress Test Preparation System put you in charge of your exam by showing you test-taking strategies that work. Practice these strategies as you take the sample tests in this book, and then you'll be ready to use them on test day.

First, take control of your time on the exam. Some law enforcement exams have a time limit, which may give you more than enough time to complete all the questions—or not enough time. It's a terrible feeling to hear the examiner say, "Five minutes left," when you're only three-quarters of the way through the test. Here are some tips to keep that from happening to you.

- **Follow directions.** If the directions are given orally, listen closely. If they're written on the exam booklet or on the computer screen (for a computerized exam), read them carefully. Ask questions *before* the exam begins if there is anything you don't understand. If you're allowed to write in your exam booklet, write down the beginning time and ending time of the exam.

- **Pace yourself.** Glance at your watch every few minutes, and compare the time to how far you've gotten in the test. When one-quarter of the time has elapsed, you should be a quarter of the way through the section, and so on. If you're falling behind, pick up the pace a bit.

- **Keep moving.** Don't waste time on one question. If you don't know the answer, skip the question and move on. Circle the number of the question in your test booklet in case you have time to come back to it later. If you're taking the exam on a computer, use scrap paper to keep track of these questions and make sure that you will be able to come back to any questions that you skip.

- **Keep track of your place on the answer sheet.** If you skip a question, make sure you skip on the answer sheet too. Check yourself every 5 to 10 questions to make sure the question number and the answer sheet number are still the same.

- **Don't rush.** Although you should keep moving, rushing won't help. Try to keep calm and work methodically and quickly.

Step 5: Learn to Use the Process of Elimination

Time to complete: 20 minutes
Activity: Complete the worksheet titled "Using the Process of Elimination."

After time management, your most important tool for taking control of your exam is using the process of elimination wisely. It's standard test-taking wisdom that you should always read all the answer choices before choosing your answer. This helps you find the right answer by eliminating wrong answer choices. And, sure enough, that standard wisdom applies to your exam, too.

Choosing the Right Answer by Process of Elimination

As you read a question, you may find it helpful to underline important information or make some notes about what you're reading. When you get to the heart of the question, circle it and make sure you understand what it is asking. If you're not sure of what's being asked, you'll never know whether you've chosen the right answer. What you do next depends on the type of question you're answering.

- Take a quick look at the answer choices for some clues. Sometimes this helps to put the question in a new perspective and makes it easier to answer. Then make a plan of attack to solve the problem.
- Otherwise, follow this simple process-of-elimination plan to manage your testing time as efficiently as possible: Read each answer choice and make a quick decision about what to do with it, marking your test book accordingly:
  ✔ The answer seems reasonable; keep it. Put a ✔ next to the answer.

  ✔ The answer is awful. Get rid of it. Put an X next to the answer.
  ✔ You can't make up your mind about the answer, or you don't understand it. Keep it for now. Put a **?** next to it.

Whatever you do, don't waste time with any one answer choice. If you can't figure out what an answer choice means, don't worry about it. If it's the right answer, you'll probably be able to eliminate all the others, and, if it's the wrong answer, another answer will probably strike you more obviously as the right answer.

- If you haven't eliminated any answers at all, skip the question temporarily, but don't forget to mark the question so you can come back to it later if you have time. If the test has no penalty for wrong answers, and you're certain that you could never answer this question in a million years, pick an answer and move on.
- If you've eliminated all but one answer, just reread the circled part of the question to make sure you're answering exactly what's asked. Mark your answer sheet and move on to the next question.
- Here's what to do when you've eliminated some, but not all of the answer choices. Compare the remaining answers looking for similarities and differences, reasoning your way through these choices. Try to eliminate those choices that don't seem as strong to you. But *don't* eliminate an answer just because you don't understand it. You may even be able to use relevant information from other parts of the test. If you've narrowed it down to a single answer, check it against the circled question to be sure you've answered it. Then mark your answer sheet and move on. If you're down to only two or three answer choices, you've improved your odds of

getting the question right. Make an educated guess and move on. However, if you think you can do better with more time, mark the question as one to return to later.

If You're Penalized for Wrong Answers

You must know whether you'll be penalized for wrong answers before you begin your law enforcement exam. If you don't, ask the proctor before the test begins. Whether you make a guess or not depends on the penalty. Some standardized tests are scored in such a way that every wrong answer reduces your score by a fraction of a point, and these can really add up against you! Whatever the penalty, if you can eliminate enough choices to make the odds of answering the question better than the penalty for getting it wrong, make a guess. This is called educated guessing.

Let's imagine you are taking a test in which each question has five choices and you are penalized one-fourth of a point for each wrong answer. If you can eliminate even one of the choices, the odds are now in your favor. If you can identify *two* of the choices as definitely wrong, you have a one in three chance of answering the question correctly. Fortunately, few tests are scored using such elaborate means, but if your test is one of them, know the penalties and calculate your odds before you take a guess on a question.

If You Finish Early

Use any time you have left to do the following:

■ Go back to questions you marked to return to later and try them again.

■ Check your work on all the other questions. If you have a good reason for thinking a response is wrong, change it.

■ Review your answer sheet. Make sure you've put the answers in the right places and you've marked only one answer for each question. (Most tests are scored in such a way that questions with more than one answer are marked wrong.)

■ If you've erased an answer, make sure you've done a good job of it.

■ Check for stray marks on your answer sheet that could distort your score.

Whatever you do, don't waste time when you've finished a test section. Make every second count by checking your work over and over again until time is called.

Try using your powers of elimination on the questions in the worksheet called "Using the Process of Elimination." The answer explanations that follow show one possible way you might use the process to arrive at the right answer.

The process of elimination is your tool for the next step, which is knowing when to guess.

Using the Process of Elimination

Use the process of elimination to answer the following questions.

1. Ilsa is as old as Meghan will be in five years. The difference between Ed's age and Meghan's age is twice the difference between Ilsa's age and Meghan's age. Ed is 29. How old is Ilsa?
   a. 4
   b. 10
   c. 19
   d. 24

2. "All drivers of commercial vehicles must carry a valid commercial driver's license whenever operating a commercial vehicle." According to this sentence, which of the following people need NOT carry a commercial driver's license?
   a. a truck driver idling his engine while waiting to be directed to a loading dock
   b. a bus operator backing her bus out of the way of another bus in the bus lot
   c. a taxi driver driving his personal car to the grocery store
   d. a limousine driver taking the limousine to her home after dropping off her last passenger of the evening

3. Smoking tobacco has been linked to
   a. an increased risk of stroke and heart attack.
   b. all forms of respiratory disease.
   c. increasing mortality rates over the past ten years.
   d. juvenile delinquency.

4. Which of the following words is spelled correctly?
   a. incorrigible
   b. outragous
   c. domestickated
   d. understandible

Answers

Here are the answers, as well as some suggestions as to how you might have used the process of elimination to find them.

1. **d.** You should have eliminated choice **a** immediately. Ilsa can't be four years old if Meghan is going to be Ilsa's age in five years. The best way to eliminate other answer choices is to try plugging them in to the information given in the problem. For instance, for choice **b**, if Ilsa is 10, then Meghan must be 5. The difference in their ages is 5. The difference between Ed's age, 29, and Meghan's age, 5, is 24. Is 24 two times 5? No. Then choice **b** is wrong. You could have eliminated choice **c** in the same way and been left with choice **d**.

2. **c.** Note the word *not* in the question, and go through the answers one by one. Is the truck driver in choice **a** "operating a commercial vehicle"? Yes, idling counts as "operating," so he needs to have a commercial driver's license. Likewise, the bus operator in choice **b** is operating a commercial vehicle; the question doesn't say the operator has to be on the street. The limo driver in choice **d** is operating a commercial vehicle, even if it doesn't have a passenger in it. However, the taxi driver in choice **c** is not operating a commercial vehicle, but his own private car.

3. a. You could eliminate choice **b** simply because of the presence of the word *all*. Such absolutes hardly ever appear in correct answer choices. Choice **c** looks attractive until you think a little about what you know—aren't fewer people smoking these days, rather than more? So how could smoking be responsible for a higher mortality rate? (If you didn't know that mortality rate means the rate at which people die, you might keep this choice as a possibility, but you'd still be able to eliminate two answers and have only two to choose from.) Choice **d** can't be proven, so you could eliminate that one, too. Now you're left with the correct choice, **a**.

4. a. How you used the process of elimination here depends on which words you recognized as being spelled incorrectly. If you knew that the correct spellings were outrageous, domesticated, and understandable, then you were home free. Surely you knew that at least one of those words was wrong.

Step 6: Know When to Guess

Time to complete: 20 minutes
Activity: Complete the worksheet "Your Guessing Ability."
Armed with the process of elimination, you're ready to take control of one of the big questions in test taking: Should I guess? The first and main answer is, it depends on the scoring rules of the test and whether you're able to eliminate any answers. Some exams have what's called a "guessing penalty," in which a fraction of your wrong answers is subtracted from your right answers. Check with the administrators of your particular exam to see if this is the case. In many instances, the number of questions you answer cor-

rectly yields your raw score. So you have nothing to lose and everything to gain by guessing.

The more complicated answer to the question, "Should I guess?" depends on you, your personality, and your guessing intuition. There are two things you need to know about yourself before you go into the exam:

1. Are you a risk taker?
2. Are you a good guesser?

You'll have to decide about your risk-taking quotient on your own. To find out if you're a good guesser, complete the worksheet called "Your Guessing Ability" that begins on this page. Frankly, even if you're a play-it-safe person with terrible intuition, you're still safe in guessing every time, as long as your exam has no guessing penalty. The best thing would be if you could overcome your anxieties and go ahead and mark an answer. But you may want to have a sense of how good your intuition is before you go into the exam.

Your Guessing Ability

The following are ten really hard questions. You're not supposed to know the answers. Rather, this is an assessment of your ability to guess when you don't have a clue. Read each question carefully, just as if you did expect to answer it. If you have any knowledge at all of the subject of the question, use that knowledge to help you eliminate wrong answer choices. Circle the letter next to the answer that represents your best guess for the right answer to each question.

1. September 7 is Independence Day in
   a. India.
   b. Costa Rica.
   c. Brazil.
   d. Australia.

2. Which of the following is the formula for determining the momentum of an object?
   a. $p = mv$
   b. $F = ma$
   c. $P = IV$
   d. $E = mc^2$

3. Because of the expansion of the universe, the stars and other celestial bodies are all moving away from each other. This phenomenon is known as
   a. Newton's first law.
   b. the big bang.
   c. gravitational collapse.
   d. Hubble flow.

4. American author Gertrude Stein was born in
   a. 1713.
   b. 1830.
   c. 1874.
   d. 1901.

5. Which of the following is NOT one of the Five Classics attributed to Confucius?
   a. the *I Ching*
   b. the *Book of Holiness*
   c. the *Spring and Autumn Annals*
   d. the *Book of History*

6. The religious and philosophical doctrine that holds that the universe is constantly in a struggle between good and evil is known as
   a. Pelagianism.
   b. Manichaeanism.
   c. neo-Hegelianism.
   d. Epicureanism.

7. The third chief justice of the U.S. Supreme Court was
   a. John Blair.
   b. William Cushing.
   c. James Wilson.
   d. John Jay.

8. Which of the following is the poisonous portion of a daffodil?
   a. the bulb
   b. the leaves
   c. the stem
   d. the flowers

9. The winner of the Masters golf tournament in 1953 was
   a. Sam Snead.
   b. Cary Middlecoff.
   c. Arnold Palmer.
   d. Ben Hogan.

10. The state with the highest per capita personal income in 1980 was
   a. Alaska.
   b. Connecticut.
   c. New York.
   d. Texas.

Answers

Check your answers against the correct answers.
   1. c.
   2. a.
   3. d.
   4. c.
   5. b.
   6. b.
   7. b.
   8. a.
   9. d.
   10. a.

How Did You Do?

You may have simply gotten lucky and actually known the answer to one or two questions. In addition, your guessing was more successful if you were able to use the process of elimination on any of the questions. Maybe you didn't know who the third chief justice was (question 7), but you knew that John Jay was the first. In that case, you would have eliminated choice **d** and therefore improved your odds of guessing right from one in four to one in three.

According to probability, you should get two and a half answers correct, so getting either two or three right would be average. If you got four or more right, you may be a really terrific guesser. If you got one or none right, you may have decided not to guess.

Keep in mind, though, that this is only a small sample. You should continue to keep track of your guessing ability as you work through the sample questions in this book. When you guess, circle the number of the questions. Remember, on a test with four answer choices, your chances of getting a right answer is one in four. So keep a separate guessing score for each exam. How many questions did you guess? How many did you get right? If the number you got right is at least one-fourth of the number of questions you guessed, you are at least an average guesser, maybe better—and you should always go ahead and guess on the real exam. If the number you got right is significantly lower than one-fourth of the number you guessed on, you should not guess on exams where there is a guessing penalty unless you can eliminate a wrong answer. If there's no guessing penalty, you would, frankly, be safe in guessing anyway.

Step 7: Reach Your Peak Performance Zone

Time to complete: 10 minutes to read; weeks to complete!
Activity: Complete the "Physical Preparation Checklist."

To get ready for a challenge like a big exam, you have to take control of your physical, as well as your mental state. Exercise, proper diet, and rest will ensure that your body works with, rather than against, your mind on test day, as well as during your preparation.

Exercise

If you don't already have a regular exercise program going, the time during which you're preparing for an exam is actually an excellent time to start one. If you're already keeping fit—or trying to get that way—don't let the pressure of preparing for an exam fool you into quitting now. Exercise helps reduce stress by pumping wonderful good-feeling hormones called endorphins into your system. It also increases the oxygen supply throughout your body and your brain, so you'll be at peak performance on test day.

A half hour of vigorous activity—enough to break a sweat—every day should be your aim. If you're really pressed for time, every other day is okay. Choose an activity you like and get out there and do it. Jogging with a friend always makes the time go faster as does listening to music.

But don't overdo it. You don't want to exhaust yourself. Moderation is the key.

Diet

First of all, cut out the junk. Go easy on caffeine and nicotine, and eliminate alcohol and any other drugs from your system at least two weeks before the exam. Promise yourself a special treat the night after the exam, if need be.

What your body needs for peak performance is simply a balanced diet. Eat plenty of fruits and vegetables, along with protein and complex carbohydrates. Foods that are high in lecithin (an amino acid), such as fish and beans, are especially good "brain foods."

Rest

You probably know how much sleep you need every night to be at your best, even if you don't always get it. Make sure you do get that much sleep, though, for at least a week before the exam. Moderation is important here, too. Extra sleep will just make you groggy.

If you're not a morning person and your exam will be given in the morning, you should reset your internal clock so that your body doesn't think you're taking an exam at 3 A.M. You have to start this process well before the exam. The way it works is to get up half an hour earlier each morning, and then go to bed half an hour earlier that night. Don't try it the other way around; you'll just toss and turn if you go to bed early without getting up early. The next morning, get up another half an hour earlier, and so on. How long you will have to do this depends on how late you're used to getting up. Use the "Physical Preparation Checklist" on this page and page 19 to make sure you're in tip-top form.

Step 8: Get Your Act Together

Time to complete: 10 minutes to read; time to complete will vary
Activity: Complete the "Final Preparations" worksheet.
Once you feel in control of your mind and body, you're in charge of test anxiety, test preparation, and test-taking strategies. Now it's time to make charts and gather the materials you need to take to the exam.

Gather Your Materials

The night before the exam, lay out the clothes you will wear and the materials you have to bring with you to the exam. Plan on dressing in layers because you won't have any control over the temperature of the exam room. Have a sweater or jacket you can take off if it's warm. Use the checklist on the worksheet entitled "Final Preparations" on pages 19 and 20 to help you pull together what you'll need.

Don't Skip Breakfast

Even if you don't usually eat breakfast, do so on exam morning. A cup of coffee doesn't count. Don't eat doughnuts or other sweet foods, either. A sugar high will leave you with a sugar low in the middle of the exam. A mix of protein and carbohydrates is best—cereal with milk or eggs with toast will do your body a world of good.

Physical Preparation Checklist

For the week before the test, write down what physical exercise you engaged in and for how long and what you ate for each meal. Remember, you're trying for at least half an hour of exercise every other day (preferably every day) and a balanced diet that's light on junk food.

Exam minus 7 days

Exercise: _____ for _____ minutes

Breakfast: _____

Lunch: _____

Dinner: _____

Snacks: _____

Exam minus 6 days

Exercise: _____ for _____ minutes

Breakfast: _____

Lunch: _____

Dinner: _____

Snacks: _____

Exam minus 5 days

Exercise: _____ for _____ minutes

Breakfast: _____

Lunch: _____

Dinner: _____

Snacks: _____

Exam minus 4 days

Exercise: _____ for _____ minutes

Breakfast: _____

Lunch: _____

Dinner: _____

Snacks: _____

Exam minus 3 days

Exercise: _____ for _____ minutes

Breakfast: _____

Lunch: _____

Dinner: _____

Snacks: _____

Exam minus 2 days

Exercise: _____ for _____ minutes

Breakfast: _____

Lunch: _____

Dinner: _____

Snacks: _____

Exam minus 1 day

Exercise: _____ for _____ minutes

Breakfast: _____

Lunch: _____

Dinner: _____

Snacks: _____

Step 9: Do It!

Time to complete: 10 minutes, plus test-taking time
Activity: Ace Your Test!

Fast-forward to exam day. You're ready. You made a study plan and followed through. You practiced your test-taking strategies while working through this book. You're in control of your physical, mental, and emotional state. You know when and where to show up and what to bring with you. In other words, you're better prepared than most of the other people taking the test with you. You're psyched!

Just one more thing. When you're finished with the exam, you will have earned a reward. Plan a night out. Call your friends and plan a party, or have a nice dinner for two—whatever your heart desires. Give yourself something to look forward to.

And then do it. Go into the exam, full of confidence, armed with test-taking strategies you've practiced until they're second nature. You're in control of yourself, your environment, and your performance on exam day. You're ready to succeed. So do it. Go in there and ace your law enforcement exam! And, then, look forward to your new career.

Final Preparations

Getting to the Exam Site

Location of exam: _____

Date of exam: _____

Time of exam: _____

Do I know how to get to the exam site?
Yes _____ No _____

If no, make a trial run.

Time it will take to get to the exam site: _____

Things to Lay Out the Night Before

Clothes I will wear   _____

Sweater/jacket   _____

Watch   _____

Photo ID   _____

Admission card   _____

Four #2 pencils   _____

_____   _____

_____   _____

3 ▶ Diagnostic Exam

se this diagnostic to gauge your strengths and weaknesses before you begin the review chapters of this book.

On this diagnostic exam, you will encounter 80 questions covering the topics you will study in Chapters 4 through 11. You should have a pencil and scrap paper handy; however, do not use a calculator.

It is not necessary to take this practice exam under timed conditions. If you choose to time yourself, however, allow about 40 minutes to complete this practice exam.

When you are finished, check the answer key on page 31 carefully to assess your results. Good luck!

1. Find the sum of 7,805 and 987.
- **a.** 17,675
- **b.** 8,972
- **c.** 8,987
- **d.** 8,792

2. $287,500 - 52,988 + 6,808 =$
 a. 347,396
 b. 46,467
 c. 333,680
 d. 241,320

3. What is the product of 450 and 122?
 a. 54,900
 b. 6,588
 c. 572
 d. 328

4. Find the quotient: $12,440 \div 40$.
 a. 497,600
 b. 12,480
 c. 12,400
 d. 311

5. When the sum of 1,352 and 731 is subtracted from 5,000, the result is
 a. 7,083
 b. 2,917
 c. 2,083
 d. 4,379

6. What is the quotient of 90 divided by 18?
 a. 5
 b. 6
 c. 72
 d. 1,620

7. $4 \times 4 \times 4 \times 4$ is equivalent to
 a. 4×4^2
 b. $4^2 \times 4^3$
 c. $(4^2)^2$
 d. $4^3 + 4^2$

8. $6^0 =$
 a. 0
 b. 1
 c. 6
 d. 60

9. $11^3 =$
 a. 121
 b. 1,331
 c. 14,641
 d. 15,551

10. What is the least common multiple of 12 and 15?
 a. 30
 b. 48
 c. 60
 d. 120

11. $4\frac{1}{3} + 3\frac{1}{3} =$
 a. $7\frac{2}{15}$
 b. $7\frac{4}{13}$
 c. $7\frac{2}{3}$
 d. $7\frac{19}{30}$

12. $\frac{1}{6} + \frac{7}{12} + \frac{2}{3} =$
 a. $\frac{10}{24}$
 b. $2\frac{1}{6}$
 c. $1\frac{5}{6}$
 d. $1\frac{5}{12}$

13. $2\frac{1}{4} + 4\frac{5}{8} + \frac{1}{2} =$
 a. $6\frac{7}{8}$
 b. $7\frac{1}{4}$
 c. $7\frac{3}{8}$
 d. $7\frac{3}{4}$

14. $\frac{1}{4} + \frac{3}{16} + \frac{7}{8} =$
 a. $1\frac{5}{16}$
 b. $\frac{11}{28}$
 c. $\frac{7}{16}$
 d. $1\frac{7}{16}$

15. $\frac{5}{9} - \frac{2}{9} =$
 a. $\frac{7}{9}$
 b. $\frac{3}{18}$
 c. $\frac{1}{3}$
 d. $\frac{2}{3}$

16. $\frac{5}{12} - \frac{7}{18} =$
  a. $\frac{1}{36}$
  b. $\frac{12}{36}$
  c. $\frac{12}{30}$
  d. $\frac{2}{6}$

17. $56\frac{3}{8} - 10\frac{5}{6} =$
  a. $46\frac{1}{7}$
  b. $46\frac{13}{14}$
  c. $45\frac{1}{3}$
  d. $45\frac{13}{24}$

18. $20\frac{5}{7} - 15\frac{1}{7} =$
  a. $5\frac{4}{14}$
  b. $5\frac{3}{7}$
  c. $5\frac{4}{7}$
  d. $5\frac{6}{7}$

19. $\frac{1}{5} \times \frac{4}{7} =$
  a. $\frac{5}{12}$
  b. $\frac{4}{35}$
  c. $\frac{1}{35}$
  d. $\frac{2}{17}$

20. $\frac{3}{4} \times \frac{16}{15} =$
  a. $\frac{5}{4}$
  b. $\frac{4}{5}$
  c. $1\frac{4}{5}$
  d. $1\frac{1}{4}$

21. Which of the following choices has a 6 in the tenths place?
  a. 60.17
  b. 76.01
  c. 1.67
  d. 7.061

22. Which of these decimals has the greatest value?
  a. 0.03
  b. 0.003
  c. 0.031
  d. 0.0031

23. $\frac{3}{20}$ is equivalent to which of the following decimals?
  a. 0.03
  b. 0.06
  c. 0.60
  d. 0.15

24. What is the sum of 8.514 and 4.821?
  a. 12.335
  b. 13.335
  c. 12.235
  d. 13.235

25. What is the sum of 3.75, 12.05, and 4.2?
  a. 20
  b. 19.95
  c. 19.00
  d. 19.75

26. What is the sum of −8.3 and 9?
  a. 17.3
  b. 0.7
  c. 1.73
  d. −17.3

27. $-6.5 - 8.32 =$
  a. 14.82
  b. 1.82
  c. −0.82
  d. −14.82

28. $0.205 \times 0.11 =$
  a. 0.02255
  b. 0.2255
  c. 2.255
  d. 22.55

29. $0.56 \times 0.03 =$
  a. 168
  b. 16.8
  c. 0.168
  d. 0.0168

30. $3.26 \div 0.02 =$

   a. 163

   b. 65.2

   c. 16.3

   d. 652

31. 15% is equivalent to which fraction?

   a. $\frac{3}{20}$

   b. $\frac{15}{1000}$

   c. $\frac{1}{5}$

   d. $\frac{1}{15}$

32. 20% is equivalent to which decimal value?

   a. 0.020

   b. 2.0

   c. 0.2

   d. 0.002

33. When converted to a decimal, 45% is equivalent to

   a. 0.045

   b. 0.45

   c. 4.5

   d. 45

34. 50% of what number equals 20% of 2,000?

   a. 200

   b. 400

   c. 600

   d. 800

35. What is 300% of 54.2?

   a. 16.26

   b. 162.6

   c. 1,626

   d. none of the above

36. What percent of $\frac{1}{2}$ is $\frac{1}{8}$?

   a. 25%

   b. 50%

   c. 80%

   d. none of the above

37. What percent of the square is shaded?

   a. 20%

   b. 37.5%

   c. 40%

   d. 80%

38. What percent of the square is shaded?

   a. 20%

   b. 37.5%

   c. 40%

   d. 80%

Use this information to answer questions 39 and 40:

Tommy has a shopping bag with 3 peaches, 4 bananas, 7 rolls, and 1 orange.

39. What is the ratio of rolls to bananas expressed as a fraction?

   a. $\frac{3}{4}$

   b. $\frac{3}{7}$

   c. $\frac{7}{1}$

   d. $\frac{7}{4}$

40. What is the ratio of peaches to the total number of items in the bag?

   a. 3 to 12

   b. 3 to 15

   c. 4 to 15

   d. 12 to 3

41. A dealer buys a car from the manufacturer for $13,000. If the dealer wants to earn a profit of 20% based on the cost, at what price should he sell the car?
   a. $16,250
   b. $15,600
   c. $15,200
   d. $10,833

42. Marla paid $14,105 for her new car. This price included 8.5% for tax. What was the price of the car excluding tax?
   a. $13,000.00
   b. $13,850.00
   c. $11,989.25
   d. $1,198.93

43. Steven's income was $34,000 last year. He must pay $2,380 for income taxes. What is the rate of taxation?
   a. 70%
   b. 7%
   c. 0.7%
   d. 0.007%

44. The supply department forgot to put the total on a recent invoice. If the cost of each of the three items was $12.56, $141.08, and $76.33, how much should the total bill be?
   a. $228.97
   b. $229.87
   c. $229.97
   d. $230.87

45. The reduced price of a computer is $1,250 after a 20% deduction is applied. The original price was then
   a. $250
   b. $1,000
   c. $1,562.50
   d. $6,250

46. Each month $68.50 is taken out of Claire's paycheck for taxes, Social Security, and other government deductions. How much money per year is being sent to the government from Claire's paychecks?
   a. $685.00
   b. $753.50
   c. $787.75
   d. $822.00

47. A construction manager is allotted $1,350 for materials on a project. The first purchase cost $579.50 and the second purchase cost $715.35. After this, $215 worth of materials was returned and then a final purchase of $275.80 took place. How much money was left over at the end?
   a. $0
   b. $5.65
   c. $7.24
   d. The manager is over budget.

48. An employer needs to keep employees from working overtime, which is anything over 40 hours in a week. If there is an employee who already has worked 9 hours on Monday, 6.5 hours on Tuesday, 8 hours on Thursday, and 10.5 hours on Friday, how many hours can the employer schedule that employee to work on Saturday?
   a. 5 hours
   b. 5.5 hours
   c. 6 hours
   d. 4.5 hours

49. You are performing an electrical job at your home, where 22 new recessed can lights will be installed. The cans come in boxes of five and the baffles (rims) come in sets of eight. How many of each should you purchase in order to have the least amount of materials left over?
   a. 4 boxes of cans and 4 boxes of baffles
   b. 5 boxes of cans and 3 boxes of baffles
   c. 6 boxes of cans and 3 boxes of baffles
   d. 8 boxes of cans and 5 boxes of baffles

50. A housekeeping company charges a flat fee of $25/house. There is an additional cost of $4.50 per room with the first room included in the flat fee. What is the total charge for cleaning two houses that have 7 rooms each?
   a. $52
   b. $104
   c. $113
   d. $175

The following graph shows the cost of yearly electricity usage for Finnigan Engineering, Inc. over the course of three years for three departments. Use this information to answer questions 51 through 54.

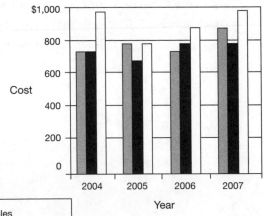

Electricity Costs

51. The electricity cost for the sales department during the year 2004 was how much greater than the electricity cost for the customer service department in 2005?
   a. $200
   b. $150
   c. $100
   d. $50

52. Which of the following statements is supported by the data?
   a. The sales department showed a steady increase in the dollar amount of electricity used during the four-year period.
   b. The customer service department showed a steady increase in the dollar amount of electricity used during the four-year period.
   c. The engineering department showed a steady increase in the dollar amount of electricity used from 2005 through 2007.
   d. none of the above

53. What was the percent decrease in electricity cost from 2004 to 2005 for the engineering department?
   a. 25%
   b. 20%
   c. 15%
   d. 10%

54. If the information in the bar graph is transcribed and a line graph is generated, which of the following line graphs is correct?

a.

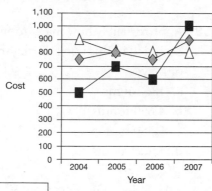

b.

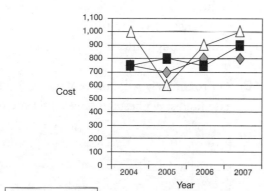

c.

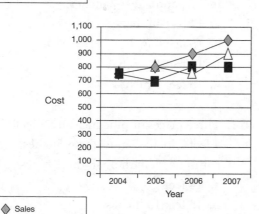

d.

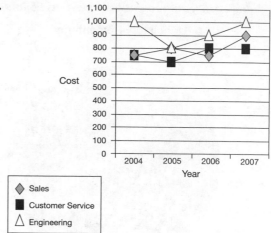

55. During 2007, at Deluxe Vacuum Co., the East and West divisions had equal sales and the North division sold the most. Which graph could be the graph of Deluxe's yearly sales for 2007?

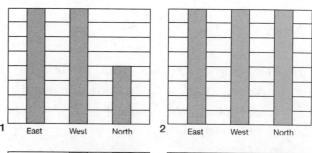

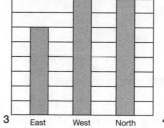
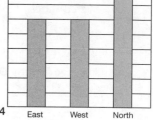

a. 1

b. 2

c. 3

d. 4

Use the circle graph to answer questions 56 and 57.

Upholstery Percentages

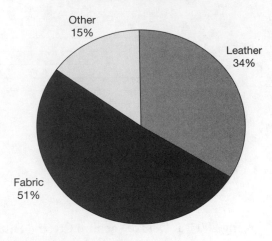

56. What is the percentage of couches that are not fabric?

   a. 15%
   b. 34%
   c. 49%
   d. 85%

57. How many couches were made in fabric if there was a total of 1,300 couches produced?

   a. 663 couches
   b. 637 couches
   c. 442 couches
   d. 212 couches

Use the bar graph to answer questions 58 through 60.

Average Nightly Occupancy by Month

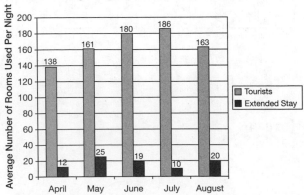

Tourists are defined as patrons who stay for one week or less. Extended stay guests are visitors who stay for more than one week.

58. Approximately how many rooms were occupied in this hotel during the entire month of May?

   a. 186 rooms
   b. 4,650 rooms
   c. 5,580 rooms
   d. 5,766 rooms

59. Which month has the highest average occupancy?

   a. June
   b. July
   c. August
   d. not enough information

60. Approximately what percentage of rooms did extended stay guests use over the time period?

   a. 7.6%
   b. 9.4%
   c. 10.4%
   d. 73.3%

61. What is the sum of 3 feet 5 inches, 10 feet 2 inches, and 2 feet 7 inches?

   a. 14 feet 14 inches
   b. 16 feet 4 inches
   c. 15 feet 13 inches
   d. 16 feet 2 inches

62. Three pieces of pipe measure 5 feet 8 inches, 4 feet 7 inches, and 3 feet 9 inches. What is the combined length of all three pipes?

   a. 14 feet
   b. 13 feet 10 inches
   c. 12 feet 9 inches
   d. 12 feet 5 inches

63. How many inches are there in $3\frac{1}{3}$ yards?
   a. 126
   b. 120
   c. 160
   d. 168

Use the following chart to answer question 64.

ENGLISH – METRIC UNIT APPROXIMATE CONVERSIONS
LENGTH
1 in. = 2.54 cm
1 yd. = .9 m
1 mi. = 1.6 km

64. 1,280 miles is equal to how many kilometers?
   a. 800 kilometers
   b. 1,152 kilometers
   c. 2,048 kilometers
   d. 3,200 kilometers

65. A child has a temperature of 40 degrees C. What is the child's temperature in degrees Fahrenheit? ($F = \frac{9}{5} C + 32$)
   a. 101°
   b. 102°
   c. 103°
   d. 104°

66. If a map drawn to scale shows 5.2 centimeters between two points and the scale is 1 cm = 1.5 km, how far away are the 2 points in meters?
   a. 7.8
   b. 780
   c. 7,800
   d. 78,000

67. Three pieces of wood measure 8 yards 2 feet 1 inch, 6 yards 1 foot 9 inches, and 3 yards 1 foot 7 inches length. When these boards are laid end to end, what is their combined length?
   a. 18 yards 17 inches
   b. 18 yards 5 feet
   c. 18 yards 2 feet 5 inches
   d. 18 yards 5 inches

68. Which of the following rope lengths is longest? (1 centimeter = 0.39 inches)
   a. 1 meter
   b. 1 yard
   c. 32 inches
   d. 85 centimeters

69. Three pieces of wood measure 4 yards 1 foot 3 inches, 5 yards 2 feet 4 inches, and 4 yards 1 foot 5 inches lengthwise. When these boards are laid end to end, what is their combined length?
   a. 14 yards 2 feet
   b. 14 yards 1 foot 11 inches
   c. 13 yards 2 inches
   d. 13 yards 2 feet

70. Three pieces of pipe measure 5 feet 8 inches, 4 feet 7 inches, and 3 feet 9 inches. What is the combined length of all three pipes?
   a. 14 feet
   b. 13 feet 10 inches
   c. 12 feet 9 inches
   d. 12 feet 5 inches

71. A rectangle has 2 sides equaling 6 feet and 1 yard, respectively. What is the area of the rectangle?
   a. 6 square feet
   b. 12 square feet
   c. 18 square feet
   d. 20 square feet

72. If the area of a circle is 9π square centimeters, what is the circumference?
- **a.** 3 centimeters
- **b.** 3π centimeters
- **c.** 9 centimeters
- **d.** 6π centimeters

73. How many 6-inch square tiles are needed to tile the floor in a rectangular room that is 12 feet long by 15 feet wide?
- **a.** 180 tiles
- **b.** 225 tiles
- **c.** 360 tiles
- **d.** 720 tiles

Refer to the following polygon to answer questions 74 and 75.

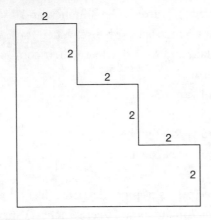

74. What is the perimeter of the polygon?
- **a.** 8 units
- **b.** 12 units
- **c.** 20 units
- **d.** 24 units

75. What is the area of the polygon?
- **a.** 8 square units
- **b.** 12 square units
- **c.** 20 square units
- **d.** 24 square units

76. A rotating door has 4 sections, labeled *a*, *b*, *c*, and *d*, as shown in the illustration. If section *a* is making a 45 degree angle with wall 1, what angle is section *c* making with wall 2?

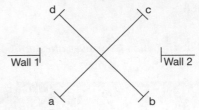

- **a.** 15 degrees
- **b.** 45 degrees
- **c.** 55 degrees
- **d.** 90 degrees

77. What is the measure of angle *C* in the following triangle?

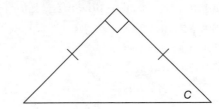

- **a.** 90°
- **b.** 60°
- **c.** 45°
- **d.** 25°

78. How much greater is the area of circle *B*?

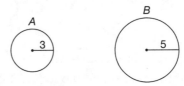

- **a.** 16π square inches
- **b.** 9π square inches
- **c.** 25π square inches
- **d.** 14π square inches

79. *ABCD* is a square and *E* is the midpoint of $\overline{AB}$. Find the area of the shaded region.

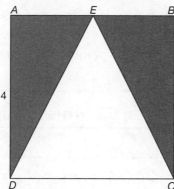

  a. 4 square units
  b. 6 square units
  c. 8 square units
  d. 12 square units

80. A square with $s = 6$ cm has the same area of a rectangle with $l = 9$ cm. What is the width of the rectangle?
  a. 4 centimeters
  b. 6 centimeters
  c. 8 centimeters
  d. 9 centimeters

Answers

1. d. *Sum* means addition, so $7{,}805 + 987 = 8{,}792$. (See Chapter 4.)

2. d. Subtract 52,988 from 287,500, which yields 234,512. Then, add 6,808 to get 241, 320. (See Chapter 4.)

3. a. To find the product, just multiply: $450 \times 122 = 54{,}900$.

4. d. 12,440 divided by 40 equals 311. Thus, the quotient is 311. (See Chapter 4.)

5. b. The sum of 1,352 and 731 is obtained by adding: $1{,}352 + 731 = 2{,}083$. Next you subtract this value from 5,000: $5{,}000 - 2{,}083 = 2{,}917$. (See Chapter 4.)

6. c. 90 divided by 18 equals 5. Thus, the quotient is 5. (See Chapter 4.)

7. c. This is 4^4 or 256 and the only answer choice that also equals 256 is $(4^2)^2$. (See Chapter 4.)

8. b. Any number (in this case 6) to the zero power is 1. (See Chapter 4.)

9. b. $11^3 = 11 \times 11 \times 11$, which equals $121 \times 11 = 1{,}331$. (See Chapter 4.)

10. c. The multiples of 12 are 12, 24, 36, 48, 60, 72, 84, 96, 108, 120. . . . The multiples of 15 are 15, 30, 45, 60, 75, 90, 105, 120. . . . Common multiples of 12 and 15 are 60 and 120, so the least common is 60. (See Chapter 4.)

11. c. When you add the whole numbers, you get 7. Both fractions have the same denominator, so you can simply add the numerators $(1 + 1)$ to get $\frac{2}{3}$. The total is $7\frac{2}{3}$. (See Chapter 5.)

12. d. First, find the least common denominator—that is, convert all three fractions to twelfths, then add: $\frac{2}{12} + \frac{7}{12} + \frac{8}{12} = \frac{17}{12}$. Now reduce: $1\frac{5}{12}$. (See Chapter 5.)

13. c. The mixed numbers must first be converted to fractions, and you must use the least common denominator, which in this case is 8. The equation then becomes: $\frac{18}{8} + \frac{37}{8} + \frac{4}{8} = \frac{59}{8}$. Now reduce: $\frac{59}{8} = 7\frac{3}{8}$. (See Chapter 5.)

14. a. First, find the least common denominator—that is, convert all three fractions to sixteenths, and then add: $\frac{4}{16} + \frac{3}{16} + \frac{14}{16} = \frac{21}{16}$. Now reduce: $1\frac{5}{16}$. (See Chapter 5.)

15. c. To add or subtract fractions, it is necessary for the fractions to share a common denominator. These two fractions have a common denominator of 9. Therefore, simply subtract the numerators and keep the denominator. The result is $\frac{3}{9}$, but in the answer choices it is expressed in lowest terms, $\frac{1}{3}$. (See Chapter 5.)

16. a. Before subtracting, you must convert both fractions to thirty-sixths: $\frac{15}{36} - \frac{14}{36} = \frac{1}{36}$. (See Chapter 5.)

17. d. First, find the common denominator, which is 24. $\frac{3}{8} = \frac{9}{24}$; $\frac{5}{6} = \frac{20}{24}$. Then convert the mixed numbers to fractions and subtract: $\frac{1,353}{24} - \frac{260}{24} = \frac{1,093}{24}$. Now change back to a mixed number: $45\frac{13}{24}$. (See Chapter 5.)

18. c. This is a basic problem of subtraction. Common errors include **d**, misreading the subtraction sign and adding the fractions instead; or **a**, subtracting the numerators but adding the denominators. (See Chapter 5.)

19. b. When multiplying fractions, multiply the numerators by each other: $1 \times 4 = 4$. Then, multiply the denominators by each other: $5 \times 7 = 35$. The correct answer is $\frac{4}{35}$.

20. b. Multiplying the numerators and denominators, you get $\frac{48}{60}$, which isn't an answer choice. However, $\frac{48}{60}$ reduces to $\frac{4}{5}$. (See Chapter 5.)

21. c. The places to the right of the decimal point are (in order): the *tenths place*, the *hundredths place*, *thousandths place*, and so on. You are looking for a 6 in the tenths place, which is the first spot to the right of the decimal point. Only choice **c** has a 6 in this place.

UNITS (ONES)	TENTHS	HUNDREDTHS
1.	6	7

Note that choice **b** has a 6 in the tens place and *not* the tenths place. (See Chapter 6.)

22. c. Choice **c** has the greatest value, $\frac{31}{1,000}$. Here is a comparison of the four choices:

a. 0.03	$\frac{3}{100} = \frac{30}{1,000}$	
b. 0.003	$\frac{3}{1,000}$	
c. 0.031	$\frac{31}{1,000}$	
d. 0.0031	$\frac{31}{10,000}$	

(See Chapter 6.)

23. d. $\frac{3}{20}$ can quickly be converted to hundredths by multiplying by $\frac{5}{5}$: $\frac{3}{20} \times \frac{5}{5} = \frac{15}{100}$. $\frac{15}{100}$ is the same as 15 *hundredths*, or 0.15, choice **d**. (See Chapter 6.)

24. b. *Sum* means *add*. Make sure you line up the decimal points and then add:

8.514
+4.821
13.335

(See Chapter 6.)

25. a. 4.2 is equivalent to 4.20. Line up all the decimal points and add:

3.75
12.05
+4.20
20.00

(See Chapter 6.)

26. b. 9 plus –8.3 is the same as 9 minus 8.3. Rewrite 9 as 9.0 and subtract:

$$\begin{array}{r} 9.0 \\ -\ 8.3 \\ \hline 0.7 \end{array}$$

(See Chapter 6.)

27. d. –6.5 – 8.32 is the same as –6.5 + –8.32. When adding 2 negative numbers, first ignore the negative signs and add in the normal fashion. 6.5 + 8.32 = 14.82. Next, insert the negative sign to get –14.82, choice **d.** (See Chapter 6.)

28. a. First multiply in the usual fashion (ignoring the decimal points): $0.205 \times 0.11 = 2,255$. Next, you need to insert the decimal point in the correct position, so take note of the position of each decimal point in the two factors:

0.205   The decimal point is **3** places to the left.

0.11   The decimal point is **2** places to the left.

In the answer, the decimal point should be **3 + 2**, or **5** places to the left. 2,255 becomes .02255, choice **a.** (See Chapter 6.)

29. d. Multiply in the usual fashion, and insert the decimal point 4 places to the left: $0.56 \times 0.03 = 168$ (when ignoring decimal) and becomes .0168 when you insert the decimal point four places to the left. Thus, the answer is choice **d.** (See Chapter 6.)

30. a. The division problem $3.26 \div 0.02$ can be solved with long division. First, just move the decimal point two places to the right in each number:

$$.02\,\overline{)\,3.26}$$

Next, divide as usual to get 163, choice **a.** (See Chapter 6.)

31. a. 15 percent equals $\frac{15}{100}$. $\frac{15}{100}$ reduces to $\frac{3}{20}$. (See Chapter 7.)

32. c. To change 20% to its equivalent decimal form, move the decimal point two places to the left. Thus, 20% = 0.20. Choice **c**, 0.2, is equivalent to 0.20. (See Chapter 7.)

33. b. When you see a percent symbol (%), you move the decimal point two places to the left. Thus, 45% is equivalent to 0.45. (See Chapter 7.)

34. d. "50% of what number equals 20% of 2,000?" can be written mathematically as $0.50 \times ? = 0.20 \times 2,000$. Dividing both sides by 0.5 will yield $? = \frac{(0.2)(2,000)}{0.5} = 800$. (See Chapter 7.)

35. b. 300% equals $\frac{300}{100}$, or 3. To find 300% of 54.2, just multiply 3 times 54.2: $3 \times 54.2 = 162.6$. (See Chapter 7.)

36. a. "What percent" can be expressed as $\frac{?}{100}$. The question "What percent of $\frac{1}{2}$ is $\frac{1}{8}$?" can be expressed as: $\frac{?}{100} \times \frac{1}{2} = \frac{1}{8}$. This simplifies to $\frac{?}{200} = \frac{1}{8}$. Cross multiplying yields $8 \times ? = 200$. Dividing both sides by 8 yields 25. (See Chapter 7.)

37. b. $\frac{3}{8}$ of the square is shaded. $3 \div 8 = 0.375$. To express this as a percent, move the decimal two places to the right: 37.5%. (See Chapter 7.)

38. b. $\frac{6}{16}$ of the square is shaded. $\frac{6}{16}$ reduces to $\frac{3}{8}$. $3 \div 8 = 0.375$. To express this as a percent, move the decimal two places to the right: 37.5%. (See Chapter 7.)

39. d. Expressed as a fraction, with the numerator equal to the first quantity and the denominator equal to the second, the ratio of rolls to bananas would be $\frac{7}{4}$. Two other ways of writing the ratio are 7 to 4, and 7:4. (See Chapter 7.)

40. b. There are 3 peaches, and $3 + 4 + 7 + 1 = 15$ items total. The ratio of peaches to the total number of items can be expressed as 3 to 15, $\frac{3}{15}$, or 3:15. (See Chapter 7.)

41. b. A 20% markup yields a new price that is 120% of the original price. $13,000 × 1.20 = $15,600. (See Chapter 8.)

42. a. If the price of the car is p, then you know that the price of the car plus 8.5% of that price added up to $14,105. 8.5% equals 0.085. Thus, $p + 0085p = 14,105$. $1.085p = 14,105$. Dividing both sides by 1.085 yields $p = \$13,000$. (See Chapter 8.)

43. b. You can solve this problem by asking yourself: "2,380 is what percent of 34,000?" and then expressing this question mathematically: $2,380 = \frac{?}{100} \times 34,000$. Divide both sides by 34,000 to get $\frac{2,380}{34,000} = \frac{?}{100}$. Cross multiply to get $238,000 = (34,000)(?)$. Divide both sides by 34,000 to get 7. Thus, the answer is 7%. (See Chapter 8.)

44. c. To find the total bill, add up the cost of the items for a total of $229.97 ($12.56 + 141.08 + 76.33 = 229.97$). (See Chapter 8.)

45. c. If a 20% deduction was applied, then $1,250 represents 80% of the original cost. This question is really asking: "80% of what is $1,250?" This can be written mathematically as $.80 \times x = 1,250$; $x = \frac{1,250}{.80} = \$1,562.50$. (See Chapter 8.)

46. d. There are 12 months in a year and each month $68.50 is held for the government. To find the total for the year, multiply the cost each month by 12 to represent an entire year ($12 \times 68.50 = \$822$). (See Chapter 8.)

47. d. Find out how much money the manager has spent and compare it to his budget ($579.50 + 715.35 - 215 + 275.80 = 1,355.65$). The manager only had $1,350, so he is over budget by $5.65 ($1,355.65 - 1,350 = 5.65$). (See Chapter 8.)

48. c. Take the total time allowed (40 hours) and subtract the time already used ($9 + 6.5 + 8 + 10.5 = 34$) to find the leftover time ($40 - 34 = 6$). (See Chapter 8.)

49. b. Find the smallest number of boxes for each part. 22 cans are needed and are sold in sets of 5, so 5 boxes are necessary (5×5 provides 25 cans). 22 baffles are also needed and they are sold in sets of 8, so only 3 boxes are necessary (3×8 provides 24 baffles). It is okay to have different amounts of each, as long as there are enough supplies for the job. (See Chapter 8.)

50. b. The final calculation is for two houses, so it may be easier to find out how much it costs to clean one house and then double it at the end. One room in the house costs $25 so the additional 6 rooms will cost $27 ($6 \times 4.50 = 27$) so the total for one house is $52 ($25 + 27 = 52$). We are trying to find the cost for two houses, so double the cost for one house to find the total cost is $104 ($52 \times 2 = 104$). (See Chapter 8.)

51. d. The sales department (black bar) spent $750 on electricity in 2004. The customer service department (white bar) spent $700 on electricity in 2005. Thus, the sales department spent $750 - $700 = $50 more. (See Chapter 9.)

52. d. None of the statements are supported by the data. Claims of steady increase over the course of four years would be visually represented as four bars, each with greater height than the prior. (See Chapter 9.)

53. b. The difference in dollar amounts used is $1,000 - $800 = $200. When compared with the original $1,000 consumed, this can be expressed as a percent by equating $\frac{200}{1,000} = \frac{x}{100}$. Thus, $x = 20\%$. (See Chapter 9.)

54. d. The line graph in choice **d** accurately displays the data that is obtained from the bar graph. (See Chapter 9.)

55. d. The East and West divisions had equal sales, so you need a graph showing the bars for East and West at the same height. North sold the most, so you need a graph that also shows North as having the largest bar in the graph. Graph 4 shows this situation. Thus, choice **d** is correct. (See Chapter 9.)

56. c. You can add up the other categories to find the percentage of couches that are not Fabric (15 + 34 = 49%). Or you can subtract the percentage that is represented by Fabric from 100% (100 − 51 = 49). (See Chapter 9.)

57. a. The object is to find 51% of the 1,300 couches. To find 51% of the 1,300 couches, simply multiply, remembering to put 51 over 100 because it represents a percentage ($1,300 \times \frac{51}{100} = 663$). (See Chapter 9.)

58. d. Rooms are used for both tourists and extended stay guests. On an average day in May there are 186 rooms used. There are 31 days in May so the rooms are used 5,766 times ($31 \times 186 = 5,766$). (See Chapter 9.)

59. a. To find the average occupancy, add up the average tourist and extended stay rooms used. In April: 150, May: 186, June: 199, July: 196, August: 183. June has the highest average. (See Chapter 9.)

60. b. To find the percentage of rooms used by extended stay guests, find out the total average over the period of time shown (12 + 25 + 19 + 10 + 20 = 86). Also, find the total number of rooms used for regular tourists (138 + 161 +180 + 186 + 163 = 828) in order to find the total number of rooms used (86 + 828 = 914). Take the rooms used by extended stay guests and divide it by the total number of rooms used and multiply it by 100 to get the percentage ($\frac{86}{914} \times 100 =$ about 9.4%). (See Chapter 9.)

61. d. First, add up all the given values:

$$
\begin{array}{rr}
3 \text{ ft.} & 5 \text{ in.} \\
10 \text{ ft.} & 2 \text{ in.} \\
+\ 2 \text{ ft.} & 7 \text{ in.} \\
\hline
15 \text{ ft.} & 14 \text{ in.}
\end{array}
$$

Next, note that 14 inches = 1 foot + 2 inches. This means 15 feet 14 inches = 16 feet 2 inches, choice **d**. (See Chapter 10.)

62. a. First, add up all the given values:

$$
\begin{array}{rr}
5 \text{ ft.} & 8 \text{ in.} \\
4 \text{ ft.} & 7 \text{ in.} \\
+\ 3 \text{ ft.} & 9 \text{ in.} \\
\hline
12 \text{ ft.} & 24 \text{ in.}
\end{array}
$$

Next, note that 24 inches = 2 feet, so 12 feet 24 inches is equivalent to 14 feet. (See Chapter 10.)

63. b. Since there arc 36 inches per yard, use the conversion factor $\frac{36 \text{ in.}}{1 \text{ yd.}}$, and multiply: $3\frac{1}{3}$ yd. $\times \frac{36 \text{ in.}}{1 \text{ yd.}} = \frac{10}{3}$ yd. $\times \frac{36 \text{ in.}}{1 \text{ yd.}} = \frac{360}{3}$ inches = 120 inches. (See Chapter 10.)

64. c. The chart says that 1 mile = about 1.6 kilometers, so you can write the conversion factor as $\frac{1.6 \text{ km}}{1 \text{ mi.}}$ and multiply: 1,280 miles $\times \frac{1.6 \text{ km}}{1 \text{ mi.}}$ = about 2,048 kilometers. (See Chapter 10.)

65. d. Substitute 40 for C in the given equation. Thus, F = $\frac{9}{5}$C + 32 becomes F = $\frac{9}{5}$(40) + 32 = (9)(8) + 32 = 72 + 32 = 104 degrees Fahrenheit. (See Chapter 10.)

66. c. First use a proportion to get the real life value: $\frac{1 \text{ cm}}{1.5 \text{ km}} = \frac{5.2 \text{ cm}}{x \text{ km}}$; $x = 1.5 \times 5.2 = 7.8$ km. Next, convert kilometers to meters by multiplying by $\frac{1,000 \text{ m}}{1 \text{ km}}$: 7.8 km $\times \frac{1,000 \text{ m}}{1 \text{ km}} =$ 7,800 m. (See Chapter 10.)

67. c. First, line up and add all the units:

8 yd. 2 ft. 1 in.
6 yd. 1 ft. 9 in.
+ 3 yd. 1 ft. 7 in.
17 yd. 4 ft. 17 in.

Next, note that 12 in. = 1 ft., so 17 yd. 4 ft. 17 in. is the same as 17 yd. 5 ft. 5 in. Next, note that 3 ft. = 1 yd., so you can rewrite the length as 18 yd. 2 ft. 5 in. (See Chapter 10.)

68. a. In order to compare the choices, convert them all into inches:

- 1 m = 100 cm = 100 cm $\times \frac{39 \text{ in.}}{\text{cm}}$ = 39 in.
- 1 yd. = 36 in.
- 32 in.
- 85 cm is less than 1 m (choice **a**) so you need not waste time converting this choice to inches.

Thus, choice **a**, 39 inches, is the longest. (See Chapter 10.)

69. a. First, line up all the units and add:

4 yd. 1 ft. 3 in.
5 yd. 2 ft. 4 in.
+ 4 yd. 1 ft. 5 in.
13 yd. 4 ft. 12 in.

Next, note that 12 in. = 1 ft., so 13 yd. 4 ft. 12 in. is the same as 13 yd. 5 ft., and that 3 ft. = 1 yd., so 5 ft. = 1 yd. + 2 ft. Ultimately, you can rewrite the entire length as 14 yd. 2 ft. (See Chapter 10.)

70. a. First, add up all the given values:

5 ft. 8 in.
4 ft. 7 in.
+ 3 ft. 9 in.
12 ft. 24 in.

Next, note that 24 in. = 2 ft., so 12 ft. 24 in. is equivalent to 14 ft. (See Chapter 10.)

71. c. First, convert the width (1 yard) into feet: 1 yard = 3 feet. Next, use $A = lw = 6 \times 3 = 18$ square feet. (Note that all the answer choices are in ft.^{2}, so converting to feet is a good idea.) (See Chapter 11.)

72. d. You are told that Area = 9π. If A = πr^2, then $\pi r^2 = 9\pi$, and $r = 3$. Circumference, $C = 2\pi r = 2\pi \times 3 = 6\pi$ centimeters. Remember that perimeters and circumferences are measured in units (like centimeters) and areas are measured in square units (like square centimeters). (See Chapter 11.)

73. d. Draw yourself a rectangle to represent the 12 feet × 15 feet floor. Since each tile is 6 inches by 6 inches, or $\frac{1}{2}$ foot by $\frac{1}{2}$ foot, you can see that you could get 24 tiles across the floor, and 30 tiles going down. Now you just multiply 24 by 30 to get the total tiles needed: $24 \times 30 = 720$. (See Chapter 11.)

74. d. Fill in the missing sides:

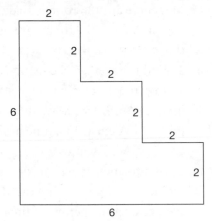

Next, add up all the sides: $P = 6 + 6 + 6(2) = 12 + 12 = 24$ units. (See Chapter 11.)

75. d. Divide the figure into squares as shown:

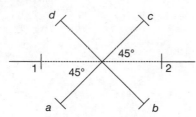

The figure is composed of 6 squares. The area of each square is $s^2 = 2^2 = 4$. Thus the total area is $6 \times 4 = 24$ square units. (See Chapter 11.)

76. b. If you draw a line on the diagram to denote the 45° angle mentioned, you can see that the angle section c makes with wall 2 must also be 45°. Recall that opposite angles formed by the intersection of two straight lines are equal:

This means that section c makes a 45° angle with wall 2. (See Chapter 11.)

77. c. The two lines through the sides of the triangle indicate that they are equal. The right angle is 90° and the 2 angles opposite the 2 equal sides will be equal. Since the interior angles of a triangle add to 180°, the 2 equal angles must add to $180° - 90° = 90°$. Thus each angle will be equal to 45°. Thus, angle $C = 45°$. (See Chapter 11.)

78. a. Remember the formula for figuring out the area of a circle: $A = \pi r^2$. Circle A then is $\pi 3^2$ or 9π and circle B is $\pi 5^2$ or 25π, so the area of circle B is 16π greater than circle A. (See Chapter 11.)

79. c. To find the area of the shaded region, simply subtract the area of the triangle from the area of the square. The area of the triangle is $\frac{1}{2} bh = \frac{1}{2}(4)(4) = 8$ square units, and the area of the square is $s^2 = 4^2 = 16$ square units. Thus, the area of the shaded region is $16 - 8 = 8$ square units. (See Chapter 11.)

80. a. The area of the square is $A = s^2 = 6^2 = 36$ square cm. The area of the rectangle must then also be 36 cm^2. Substituting this into the area formula, along with $l = 9$ we get: $A = lw$; $36 = 9 \times w$; $w = 36 \div 9 = 4$ cm. (See Chapter 11.)

4 ▶ Arithmetic Review

T his chapter covers the basics of numbers, mathematical operations, and their sequence.

Introduction to Numbers

Whole numbers include the counting numbers and zero:

0, 1, 2, 3, 4, 5, 6, . . .

Integers include the whole numbers and their opposites. Remember, the opposite of zero is zero:

. . . −3, −2, −1, 0, 1, 2, 3, . . .

An integer can be either greater than 0, called positive, or less than 0, called negative. Zero is neither positive nor negative.

When letters are used to represent numbers, the letters are called **variables**. These letters are known as variables because the numbers they represent can vary—that is, you can substitute one or more numbers for the letters in the expression:

x, y, s

You can compare numbers by determining whether one of the numbers is greater than, less than, or equal to the other number. The following table illustrates some comparison symbols.

$=$	is equal to	$5 = 5$
$\neq$	is not equal to	$4 \neq 3$
$>$	is greater than	$5 > 3$
$\geq$	is greater than or equal to (the variable x can be 5 or any number > 5)	$x \geq 5$
$<$	is less than	$-4 < 6$
$\leq$	is less than or equal to (the variable x can be 3 or any number < 3)	$x \leq 3$

Symbols of Addition

Addition is used when it is necessary to combine amounts. In addition, the numbers being added are called *addends*. The result is called a *sum*. The symbol for addition is called a *plus sign*. In the following example, 4 and 5 are addends and 9 is the sum:

$4 + 5 = 9$

Symbols of Subtraction

Subtraction is the mathematical opposite of addition. Instead of combining one number with another, you take one away from another. In subtraction, the number being subtracted is called the *subtrahend*. The number being subtracted *from* is called the *minuend*. The answer to a subtraction problem is called a *difference*. The symbol for subtraction is called a *minus sign*. In the following example, 15 is the minuend, 4 is the subtrahend, and 11 is the difference.

$15 - 4 = 11$

Symbols of Multiplication

When two or more numbers are being multiplied, they are called *factors*. The answer that results is called the *product*. In the following example, 5 and 6 are factors and 30 is their product.

$5 \times 6 = 30$

There are several ways to represent multiplication in the previous mathematical statement:

- A dot between factors indicates multiplication:
  $5 \cdot 6 = 30$
- Parentheses around any one or more factors indicate multiplication:
  $(5)6 = 30, 5(6) = 30,$ and $(5)(6) = 30$
- Multiplication is also indicated when a number is placed next to a variable:
  $5a = 30$ (In this equation, 5 is being multiplied by a.)

Symbols of Division

In division, the number being divided *by* is called the *divisor*. The number being divided *into* is called the *dividend*. The answer to a division problem is called the *quotient*.

There are a few different ways to represent division with symbols. In each of the following equivalent expressions, 3 is the divisor and 8 is the dividend:

$$8 \div 3 \qquad {}^{8}\!/_{3} \qquad \frac{8}{3} \qquad 3\overline{)8}$$

Operations

Addition

Basic problem solving in mathematics is rooted in whole number math facts, mainly addition facts and multiplication tables (for the multiplication table see page 53). One important step to mastering addition is to know how to flash on the single-digit adding facts, like $5 + 2 = 7$. If you are unsure of any of these facts, now is the time to review.

Practice

Fill in the addition facts in the table that follows without using a calculator.

1.

ZERO				
0 + 0 =	0 + 1 =	0 + 2 =	0 + 3 =	0 + 4 =
0 + 5 =	0 + 6 =	0 + 7 =	0 + 8 =	0 + 9 =

ONE				
1 + 0 =	1 + 1 =	1 + 2 =	1 + 3 =	1 + 4 =
1 + 5 =	1 + 6 =	1 + 7 =	1 + 8 =	1 + 9 =

TWO				
2 + 0 =	2 + 1 =	2 + 2 =	2 + 3 =	2 + 4 =
2 + 5 =	2 + 6 =	2 + 7 =	2 + 8 =	2 + 9 =

THREE				
3 + 0 =	3 + 1 =	3 + 2 =	3 + 3 =	3 + 4 =
3 + 5 =	3 + 6 =	3 + 7 =	3 + 8 =	3 + 9 =

FOUR				
4 + 0 =	4 + 1 =	4 + 2 =	4 + 3 =	4 + 4 =
4 + 5 =	4 + 6 =	4 + 7 =	4 + 8 =	4 + 9 =

FIVE				
5 + 0 =	5 + 1 =	5 + 2 =	5 + 3 =	5 + 4 =
5 + 5 =	5 + 6 =	5 + 7 =	5 + 8 =	5 + 9 =

SIX				
6 + 0 =	6 + 1 =	6 + 2 =	6 + 3 =	6 + 4 =
6 + 5 =	6 + 6 =	6 + 7 =	6 + 8 =	6 + 9 =

SEVEN				
7 + 0 =	7 + 1 =	7 + 2 =	7 + 3 =	7 + 4 =
7 + 5 =	7 + 6 =	7 + 7 =	7 + 8 =	7 + 9 =

EIGHT				
8 + 0 =	8 + 1 =	8 + 2 =	8 + 3 =	8 + 4 =
8 + 5 =	8 + 6 =	8 + 7 =	8 + 8 =	8 + 9 =

NINE				
9 + 0 =	9 + 1 =	9 + 2 =	9 + 3 =	9 + 4 =
9 + 5 =	9 + 6 =	9 + 7 =	9 + 8 =	9 + 9 =

TEN				
10 + 0 =	10 + 1 =	10 + 2 =	10 + 3 =	10 + 4 =
10 + 5 =	10 + 6 =	10 + 7 =	10 + 8 =	10 + 9 =
10 + 10 =				

HERE'S A TIP

When working with single-digit addition facts, there are several rules to keep in mind.

Zero plus a whole number always equals that number.

$0 + 8 = 8$

$0 + 9 = 9$

One plus a whole number is equal to the next whole number.

$1 + 8 = 9$

$1 + 9 = 10$

Two plus a number is like counting twice from that number. You will always end up on the next odd or even number, depending on whether the original number was odd or even.

$8 + 2 = 10$ (10 is the next even number after 8.)

$3 + 2 = 5$ (5 is the next odd number after 3.)

It is sometimes easier to add using tens, when possible. For example, when adding nine plus a number, bump the nine up one, to 10, and bump the other number down one.

$9 + 7 = 10 + 6 = 16$

When adding eight plus a number, bump the eight up two, to 10, and bump the other number down two.

$8 + 7 = 10 + 5 = 15$

Bump one number up to 10 and the other number down whenever it is convenient.

$7 + 6 = 10 + 3 = 13$

Make sure to memorize any parts of this review that you find troublesome. Your ability to work with numbers depends on how quickly and accurately you can do simple addition computations.

It is easiest to add multi-digit numbers when the addends are stacked in a column with the place values aligned. Work from right to left, starting with the ones column.

Example

Add $40 + 129 + 24$.

1. Align the addends in the ones column. Since it is necessary to work from right to left, begin to add with the digits in the ones column. The ones column totals 13, and 13 equals 1 ten and 3 ones, so write the 3 in the ones column of the answer, and regroup or "carry" the 1 ten to top of the tens column so it gets added with the other tens:

$$
\begin{array}{r}
{}^{1} \\
40 \\
129 \\
+\ \ 24 \\
\hline
3
\end{array}
$$

2. Add the digits in the tens column, including the regrouped 1.

$$
\begin{array}{r}
{}^{1} \\
40 \\
129 \\
+\ \ 24 \\
\hline
93
\end{array}
$$

3. Then add the digits in the hundreds column. Since there is only one value, write the 1 in the answer.

$$
\begin{array}{r}
{}^{1} \\
40 \\
129 \\
+\ \ 24 \\
\hline
193
\end{array}
$$

Practice

Use addition to solve the following problems without using a calculator.

2. Lawrence gave $281 to Joel. If Joel originally had $1,375, how much money does he have now?

3. Peter had $10,573 in his savings account. He then deposited $2,900 and $317. How much is in the account now?

4. $7 + 3 =$

5. $62 + 7 =$

6. $25 + 16 =$

7. $23 + 22 =$

Subtraction

Subtraction is used to find the difference between amounts. It is easiest to subtract when the minuend and subtrahend are in a column with the place values aligned. Again, just as in addition, work from right to left. It may be necessary to regroup.

Example

If Officer Giada has 52 arrests, and Officer Smith has 36 arrests, how many more arrests does Officer Giada have?

1. Find the difference between their arrest numbers by subtracting. Start with the ones column. Since 2 is less than the number being subtracted (6), regroup or "borrow" a ten from the tens column. Add the regrouped amount to the ones column. Now subtract $12 - 6$ in the ones column.

$$\begin{array}{r} {}^{4}\cancel{5}{}^{1}2 \\ -\ 36 \\ \hline 6 \end{array}$$

2. Regrouping 1 ten from the tens column left 4 tens. Subtract $4 - 3$ and write the result in the tens column of the answer. Officer Giada has 16 more arrests than Officer Smith.

$$\begin{array}{r} {}^{4}\cancel{5}{}^{1}2 \\ -\ 36 \\ \hline 16 \end{array}$$

3. Check: $16 + 36 = 52$.

$$\begin{array}{r} {}^{1}\ \\ 16 \\ +\ 36 \\ \hline 52 \end{array}$$

Practice

Use subtraction to solve the following problems without using a calculator.

8. $9 - 2 =$

9. $54 - 17 =$

10. $39 - 18 =$

11. $36,785 - 188 =$

Use addition and subtraction to solve the following problems.

12. $72 + 98 - 17 =$

13. $376 - 360 + 337 =$

Multiplication

In multiplication, the same amount is combined multiple times. For example, instead of adding 30 three times, $30 + 30 + 30$, it is easier to simply multiply 30 by 3. If a problem asks for the product of two or more numbers, the numbers should be multiplied together.

HERE'S A TIP

Here are some strategies to help you quickly determine single-digit multiplication facts:

- Zero times any number is zero.
  $0 \times 8 = 0$

- One times any number is that number.
  $1 \times 8 = 8$

- Two times any number is that number plus itself.
  $2 \times 8 = 8 + 8 = 16$

- Three times any number is the number plus the double of the number.
  $3 \times 8 = 8 \times 2 + 8 = 8 + 16 = 24$

- Four times any number can be calculated by doubling the number, and then doubling that number (because $4 = 2 \times 2$). To calculate 4×7, double the 7 to get 14 and double the 14 to get 28.

- Five times any even number is like taking half the number and then multiplying by ten. For 5×8, take half of 8 to get 4 and then and multiply 4 by 10 to get 40.

- Six times any number can be calculated by tripling the number and then doubling that number (because $6 = 3 \times 2$). For 6×8, triple the 8 to get 24, and then double 24 to get 48.

- Eight times any number can be found by doubling the number and then doubling that number and then doubling once again. To calculate 8×6: double the 6 to get 12, then double the 12 to get 24, and then double the 24 to get 48.

- Nine times any number can be calculated by tripling the number and then tripling that number. Triple 9 to get 27 and then triple 27 to get 81.

Do you know the multiplication facts table by heart? Many people have become so dependent on their calculators that they've forgotten a few multiplication problems—like 9×6 or 8×7.

Practice

14. Complete this multiplication facts table without using a calculator.

×	0	1	2	3	4	5	6	7	8	9	10
0	0	0	0								
1	0	1	2								
2	0	2	4								
3				9	12						
4											
5											
6											
7											
8											
9											
10											

Let's look at a multiplication problem that uses multi-digit numbers.

Example
Find the product of 34 and 54.

1. Line up the place values vertically, writing the problem in columns. Multiply the number in the ones place of the top factor (4) by the number in the ones place of the bottom factor (4): $4 \times 4 = 16$. Since $16 = 1$ ten and 6 ones, write the 6 in the ones place in the product. Regroup, or carry,

the ten by writing a 1 above the tens place of the top factor.

$$\begin{array}{r} {}^{1} \\ 34 \\ \times\ 54 \\ \hline 6 \end{array}$$

2. Multiply the number in the tens place in the top factor (3) by the number in the ones place of the bottom factor (4). $4 \times 3 = 12$. Then add the regrouped amount $12 + 1 = 13$. Write the 3 in the tens column and the one in the hundreds column of the product.

$$\begin{array}{r} {}^{1} \\ 34 \\ \times\ 54 \\ \hline 136 \end{array}$$

3. The last calculations to be done require multiplying by the tens place of the bottom factor. Multiply 5 (tens from bottom factor) by 4 (ones from top factor). $5 \times 4 = 20$, but since the 5 really represents a number of tens, the actual value of the answer is 200 (because $50 \times 4 = 200$). Therefore, write the two zeros under the ones and tens columns of the second partial product and regroup, or carry, the 2 hundreds by writing a 2 above the tens place of the top factor.

$$\begin{array}{r} {}^{2} \\ 34 \\ \times\ 54 \\ \hline 136 \\ 00 \end{array}$$

4. Multiply the 5 tens from bottom factor by the 3 tens from top factor. $5 \times 3 = 15$, but since the 5 and the 3 each represent a number of tens, the actual value of the answer is 1,500 (because $50 \times 30 = 1,500$). Add the two additional hundreds carried over from the last multiplication: $15 + 2 = 17$ (hundreds). Write the 17 in front of the zeros in the second partial product.

$$\begin{array}{r} {}^{2} \\ 34 \\ \times\ 54 \\ \hline 136 \\ 1,700 \end{array}$$

5. Add the partial products to find the total product:

$$\begin{array}{r} {}^{2} \\ 34 \\ \times\ 54 \\ \hline 136 \\ +\ 1,700 \\ \hline 1,836 \end{array}$$

Practice

Use multiplication to solve the following problems without using a calculator.

15. $46 \times 37 =$

16. $89 \times 57 =$

17. Express $5 + 5 + 5 + 5 + 5 + 5 + 5 + 5$ as a multiplication problem and give the result.

18. $348 \times 624 =$

19. A corrections officer is overseeing 17 inmates in each of 7 separate cell blocks. How many inmates is he overseeing altogether?

Division

In division, the same amount is subtracted multiple times. For example, instead of subtracting 5 from 25 as many times as possible, $25 - 5 - 5 - 5 - 5 - 5$, it is easier to simply divide, asking how many 5s are in 25: $25 \div 5$.

Example

To study for a law enforcement exam, 3 candidates pooled their money to buy a study guide for $54. If they each put in an equal amount, how much did each candidate pay?

1. Divide the total amount ($54) by the number of ways the money is to be split (3). Work from left to right. How many times does 3 divide into 5? Write the answer, 1, directly above the 5 in the dividend, since both the 5 and the 1 represent a number of tens. Now multiply: since 1 (ten) $\times$ 3 (ones) = 3 (tens), write the 3 under the 5, and subtract. 5(tens) $-$ 3(tens) = 2(tens).

$$\begin{array}{r} 1 \\ 3\overline{)54} \\ \underline{-3} \\ 2 \end{array}$$

2. Continue dividing. Bring down the 4 from the ones place in the dividend. How many times does 3 divide into 24? Write the answer, 8, directly above the 4 in the dividend. Since $3 \times 8 = 24$, write 24 below the other 24 and subtract $24 - 24 = 0$.

$$\begin{array}{r} 18 \\ 3\overline{)54} \\ \underline{-3}\downarrow \\ 24 \\ \underline{-24} \\ 0 \end{array}$$

3. If you get a number other than zero after your last subtraction, this number is your remainder.

Try another division problem:

Example

Find 9 divided by 4.

$$\begin{array}{r} 2 \\ 4\overline{)9} \\ \underline{-8} \\ 1 \end{array}$$

1 is the remainder
The answer is 2 r1.

Practice

Use division to solve the following problems without using a calculator.

20. $8 \div 2 =$

21. $7\overline{)2,114}$

22. $9\overline{)413}$

23. $596 \div 37 =$

24. 150,000 divided by 52 is ___ with a remainder of ___.

Factors and Multiples

Factors are numbers that can be divided into a whole number without a remainder.

Example

$12 \div 3 = 4$

   The number 3 is, therefore, a factor of the number 12. Other factors of 12 are 1, 2, 4, 6, and 12. The common factors of two numbers are the factors that both numbers have in common.

Example

The factors of 24 = 1, 2, 3, 4, 6, 8, 12, and 24.

   The factors of 18 = 1, 2, 3, 6, 9, and 18.

   From the preceding, you can see that the common factors of 24 and 18 are 1, 2, 3, and 6. From this list it can also be determined that the *greatest* common factor of 24 and 18 is 6.

   Multiples are numbers that can be obtained by multiplying a number x by a positive integer.

Example

$5 \times 7 = 35$

   The number 35 is, therefore, a multiple of the number 5 and of the number 7. Other multiples of 5 are 5, 10, 15, 20, etc. Other multiples of 7 are 7, 14, 21, 28, etc.

   The common multiples of two numbers are the multiples that both numbers share.

Example

Some multiples of 4 are: 4, 8, 12, 16, 20, 24, 28, 32, 36, . . .

   Some multiples of 6 are: 6, 12, 18, 24, 30, 36, 42, . . .

   Some common multiples are 12, 24, and 36. From the preceding it can also be determined that the *least* common multiple of the numbers 4 and 6 is 12, since this number is the smallest number that appeared in both lists.

Practice

Circle the numbers that have the factor 9. Underline the multiples of 2. Draw a square around the numbers that have the factor 6.

25. 4

26. 5

27. 7

28. 12

29. 13

30. 17

31. 21

32. 25

33. 29

34. 36

35. 44

36. 53

37. 81

38. 90

Working with Integers

Remember, an integer is a whole number or its opposite. Here are some rules for working with integers:

Adding

Adding numbers with the same sign results in a sum of the same sign:

(pos) + (pos) = pos   and   (neg) + (neg) = neg

When adding numbers of different signs, follow this two-step process:

1. Subtract the positive values of the numbers. Positive values are the values of the numbers without any signs.
2. Keep the sign of the number with the larger value.

Example

$-2 + 3 =$

1. Subtract the positive values of the numbers: $3 - 2 = 1$
2. The number 3 is the larger of the two positive values. Its sign in the original example was positive, so the sign of the answer is positive. The answer is positive 1, or 1.

Example

$8 + -11 =$

1. Subtract the positive values of the numbers: $11 - 8 = 3$
2. The number 11 is the larger of the two positive values. Its sign in the original example was negative, so the sign of the answer is negative. The answer is negative 3, or -3.

Subtracting

When subtracting integers, change all subtraction signs to addition signs and change the sign of the number being subtracted to its opposite. Then follow the rules for addition.

Examples

$(+10) - (+12) = (+10) + (-12) = -2$
$(-5) - (-7) = (-5) + (+7) = +2$

Practice

Solve the following problems without using a calculator.

39. $17 + -4 =$

40. $174 + 58 =$

41. $-1,023 + 75 =$

42. $99 - 16 =$

43. $-3 - -5 =$

44. $-59 - 18 =$

Multiplying and Dividing

If the signs are the same when multiplying or dividing two quantities, the answer will be positive. If the signs are different, the answer will be negative.

(pos) × (pos) = pos   (pos) ÷ (pos) = pos
(pos) × (neg) = neg   (pos) ÷ (neg) = neg
(neg) × (neg) = pos   (neg) ÷ (neg) = pos

Examples

$(10)(-12) = -120$
$-5 \times -7 = 35$
$-12 \div 3 = -4$
$15 \div 3 = 5$

Practice

Solve the following problems without using a calculator.

45. $9 \times 7 =$

46. $-15 \times -3 =$

47. $100 \times -3 =$

48. $125 \div 25 =$

49. $-81 \div -9 =$

50. $-258 \div 3 =$

Properties of Arithmetic

Listed here are several properties of mathematics:

- *Commutative Property:* This property states that the order of numbers in multiplication or addition can be changed without changing the outcome.

  Examples

  $5 \times 2 = 2 \times 5$
  $(5)(a) = (a)(5)$
  $b + 3 = 3 + b$

- *Associative Property:* This property states that parentheses can be moved to group numbers differently when adding or multiplying without affecting the answer.

  Examples

  $2 + (3 + 4) = (2 + 3) + 4$
  $2(ab) = (2a)b$

- *Distributive Property:* When a value is being multiplied by a sum or difference, multiply that value by each quantity within the parentheses and then take the sum or difference.

Examples

$5(a + b) = 5a + 5b$
$5(100 - 6) = (5 \times 100) - (5 \times 6)$

This second example can be proved by performing the calculations:

$5(94) = 500 - 30$
$470 = 470$

Powers

When you raise a number (the base) to an exponent, this is sometimes called raising the number to a **power**.

$\text{Base}^{\text{power}}$ or $\text{Base}^{\text{exponent}}$

An exponent indicates the number of times a base is used as a factor to attain a product.

Example

$2^5 = ?$

In 2^5, 2 is the base and 5 is the exponent. Therefore, 2 should be used as a factor 5 times to attain a product:

$2^5 = 2 \times 2 \times 2 \times 2 \times 2 = 32$

It's possible for a variable to have an exponent:

b^n

The b represents a number that will be a factor to itself n times.

Example

Find the value of b^n if $b = 5$ and $n = 3$.
$b^n = 5^3 = 5 \times 5 \times 5 = 125$

HERE'S A TIP

Don't let the variables become intimidating. Most expressions are very simple once numbers have been substituted for the variables.

Any base to the zero power is always 1.

Examples

$5^0 = 1$

$70^0 = 1$

$29,874^0 = 1$

Two common powers have special names. When raising a number to the second power, it is called **squaring** the number: 3 to the second power $= 3^2 = 9$. When raising a number to the third power, it is called **cubing** the number: 3 to the third power $= 3^3 = 27$.

Operations with Exponents

If the terms have different bases, you cannot combine them. When you have the same base, it is easy to combine the exponents according to the following rules:

- When multiplying like bases, such as $a^x \times a^y$, simply add the exponents: $a^x \times a^y = a^{x+y}$
- When dividing, such as $a^x \div a^y$, simply subtract the exponents: $a^x \div a^y = a^{x-y}$
- When raising a power to a power, such as $(a^x)^y$, simply multiply the exponents: $(a^x)^y = a^{xy}$
- If one of the bases doesn't have an exponent written, that means its exponent is 1: $a = a^1$
- Note that if more than one base is included in the parentheses, you must raise all the bases to the power outside the parentheses, so $(a^x b^y)^z = a^{xz} b^{yz}$.

Example

Solve $(6^2)^5$.

1. Remember, when raising a power to a power, you can just multiply the exponents. Here, multiply 2×5: $(6^2)^5 = 6^{2 \times 5} = 6^{10}$

2. You can check your work by writing out the solution: $(6^2)^5 = (6 \times 6)^5 = (6 \times 6)(6 \times 6)(6 \times 6)$ $(6 \times 6)(6 \times 6)$
   This is 6 to the tenth power, or 6^{10}.

Practice

Solve the following problems without using a calculator.

51. Evaluate 6^4.

52. Circle the expression that is NOT equivalent to $5 \cdot 5 \cdot 5 \cdot 5$.

   $5 \cdot 4$

   $(5 \cdot 5)^2$

   5^4

   $5 \cdot 5^3$

   625

53. Evaluate $cd^2 - 1$ when $c = -1$ and $d = -6$.

54. Four to the second power is equivalent to _____.

55. Evaluate $2^2 \cdot 2^3$.

56. Simplify: $a^2 b \cdot ab^3$.

57. Simplify: $x^6 \div x^3$.

58. Simplify $(3xy^3)^2$.

Sequence of Mathematical Operations

There is an order in which a sequence of mathematical operations must be performed:

- **P:** **Parentheses/Grouping Symbols.** Perform all operations within parentheses first. If there is more than one set of parentheses, begin to work with the innermost set and work toward the outside. If more than one operation is present within the parentheses, use the remaining rules of order to determine which operation to perform first.
- **E:** **Exponents.** Evaluate exponents.
- **M/D:** **Multiply/Divide.** Work from left to right in the expression.
- **A/S:** **Add/Subtract.** Work from left to right in the expression.

This order is illustrated by the acronym PEMDAS, which can be remembered by using the first letter of each of the words in the phrase: Please Excuse My Dear Aunt Sally. You can also create your own phrase, like Police Examine Many Details At Scenes.

Example

$$\frac{(5+3)^2}{4} + 27 = \frac{(8)^2}{4} + 27$$

$$= \frac{64}{4} + 27$$

$$= 16 + 27$$

$$= 43$$

You may be wondering why you really need to follow the order of operations. Look at what happens when you ignore PEMDAS and attack a problem in order of appearance:

$9 + 8 \times 2 - 3 \times 2$

$17 \times 2 - 3 \times 2$

$34 - 3 \times 2$

31×2

62

Because you ignored PEMDAS, this is not the right answer. Now solve the same problem by using the order of operations. There are no parentheses or exponents, so you need to do any multiplication or division first from left to right.

$9 + \mathbf{8 \times 2} - 3 \times 2$

$9 + 16 - \mathbf{3 \times 2}$

$9 + 16 - 6$

Now, complete the addition and subtraction from left to right.

$\mathbf{9 + 16} - 6$

$\mathbf{25 - 6}$

19

Without using the order of operations, the answer wasn't even close to the actual value. Remember, take your time and carry out each operation in the correct order.

Practice

Solve the following problems with PEMDAS without using a calculator.

59. $2^2 + (6-5) - (3+3) \times 3 =$

60. $8 + 15 \times 3 =$

61. $7 + 24 \div 6 \times 10 =$

62. $(36 + 64) \div (18 - 20) =$

Answers

1.

ZERO				
0 + 0 = 0	0 + 1 = 1	0 + 2 = 2	0 + 3 = 3	0 + 4 = 4
0 + 5 = 5	0 + 6 = 6	0 + 7 = 7	0 + 8 = 8	0 + 9 = 9

ONE				
1 + 0 = 1	1 + 1 = 2	1 + 2 = 3	1 + 3 = 4	1 + 4 = 5
1 + 5 = 6	1 + 6 = 7	1 + 7 = 8	1 + 8 = 9	1 + 9 = 10

TWO				
2 + 0 = 2	2 + 1 = 3	2 + 2 = 4	2 + 3 = 5	2 + 4 = 6
2 + 5 = 7	2 + 6 = 8	2 + 7 = 9	2 + 8 = 10	2 + 9 = 11

THREE				
3 + 0 = 3	3 + 1 = 4	3 + 2 = 5	3 + 3 = 6	3 + 4 = 7
3 + 5 = 8	3 + 6 = 9	3 + 7 = 10	3 + 8 = 11	3 + 9 = 12

FOUR				
4 + 0 = 4	4 + 1 = 5	4 + 2 = 6	4 + 3 = 7	4 + 4 = 8
4 + 5 = 9	4 + 6 = 10	4 + 7 = 11	4 + 8 = 12	4 + 9 = 13

FIVE				
5 + 0 = 5	5 + 1 = 6	5 + 2 = 7	5 + 3 = 8	5 + 4 = 9
5 + 5 = 10	5 + 6 = 11	5 + 7 = 12	5 + 8 = 13	5 + 9 = 14

SIX				
6 + 0 = 6	6 + 1 = 7	6 + 2 = 8	6 + 3 = 9	6 + 4 = 10
6 + 5 = 11	6 + 6 = 12	6 + 7 = 13	6 + 8 = 14	6 + 9 = 15

SEVEN				
7 + 0 = 7	7 + 1 = 8	7 + 2 = 9	7 + 3 = 10	7 + 4 = 11
7 + 5 = 12	7 + 6 = 13	7 + 7 = 14	7 + 8 = 15	7 + 9 = 16

EIGHT				
8 + 0 = 8	8 + 1 = 9	8 + 2 = 10	8 + 3 = 11	8 + 4 = 12
8 + 5 = 13	8 + 6 = 14	8 + 7 = 15	8 + 8 = 16	8 + 9 = 17

NINE				
9 + 0 = 9	9 + 1 = 10	9 + 2 = 11	9 + 3 = 12	9 + 4 = 13
9 + 5 = 14	9 + 6 = 15	9 + 7 = 16	9 + 8 = 17	9 + 9 = 18

TEN				
10 + 0 = 10	10 + 1 = 11	10 + 2 = 12	10 + 3 = 13	10 + 4 = 14
10 + 5 = 15	10 + 6 = 16	10 + 7 = 17	10 + 8 = 18	10 + 9 = 19
10 + 10 = 20				

2. $1,656

3. $13,790

4. 10

5. 69

6. 41

7. 45

8. 7

9. 37

10. 21

11. 36,597

12. 153

13. 353

14.

×	0	1	2	3	4	5	6	7	8	9	10
0	0	0	0	0	0	0	0	0	0	0	0
1	0	1	2	3	4	5	6	7	8	9	10
2	0	2	4	6	8	10	12	14	16	18	20
3	0	3	6	9	12	15	18	21	24	27	30
4	0	4	8	12	16	20	24	28	32	36	40
5	0	5	10	15	20	25	30	35	40	45	50
6	0	6	12	18	24	30	36	42	48	54	60
7	0	7	14	21	28	35	42	49	56	63	70
8	0	8	16	24	32	40	48	56	64	72	80
9	0	9	18	27	36	45	54	63	72	81	90
10	0	10	20	30	40	50	60	70	80	90	100

15. 1,702

16. 5,073

17. $5 \times 8 = 40$

18. 217,152

19. The corrections officer is overseeing 119 inmates.

20. 4

21. 302

22. 45 R8

23. 16 R4

24. 150,000 divided by 52 is 2,884 with remainder 32.

25. 4 __

26. 5

27. 7

28. 12 __ □

29. 13

30. 17

31. 21

32. 25

33. 29

34. 36 __ ○□

35. 44 __

36. 53

37. 81 ○

38. 90 __ ○□

39. 13

40. 232

41. −948

42. 83

43. 2

44. −77

45. 63

46. 45

47. −300

48. 5

49. 9

50. −86

51. 1,296

52. 5 · 4 should be circled

53. −37

54. 16

55. 2^5 or 32

56. a^3b^4

57. x^3

58. $9x^2y^6$

59. −13

60. 53

61. 47

62. −50

5 ▶ Fractions

T his chapter covers adding, subtracting, multiplying, dividing, and comparing fractions.

A **fraction** is a part of something (a whole). Fractions are written as $\frac{\text{part}}{\text{whole}}$, or more technically as $\frac{\text{numerator}}{\text{denominator}}$. Take a look at three kinds of fractions:

Proper fraction:

$\frac{1}{2}, \frac{2}{3}, \frac{4}{9}, \frac{8}{13}$

In a proper fraction, the top number is less than the bottom number. The value of a proper fraction is less than 1.

Improper fraction:

$\frac{3}{2}, \frac{5}{3}, \frac{14}{9}, \frac{12}{12}$

In an improper fraction, the top number is greater than or equal to the bottom number. The value of an improper fraction is 1 or more.

Mixed number:

$3\frac{1}{2}; 4\frac{2}{3}; 12\frac{3}{4}; 24\frac{3}{4}$

In a mixed number, a fraction is written to the right of a whole number. The value of a mixed number is more than 1; it is the sum of the whole number plus the fraction.

Practice

Label each fraction as "proper," "improper," or "mixed."

1. $\frac{10}{9}$

2. $\frac{1}{2}$

3. $\frac{99}{99}$

4. $15\frac{7}{8}$

Changing Improper Fractions into Mixed or Whole Numbers

Some math questions may ask you to convert an improper fraction into a mixed number.

Example

$\frac{13}{2}$

1. Divide the denominator (2) into the numerator (13) to get the whole number portion (6) of the mixed number: $13 \div 2 = 6$ r1.

2. Write the remainder of the division (1) over the old denominator (2): $6\frac{1}{2}$

3. Check: Change the mixed number back into an improper fraction (see steps in the next section).

Practice

Convert each improper fraction to a mixed number. Write your answers in simplest form.

5. $\frac{15}{2}$

6. $\frac{22}{6}$

7. $\frac{50}{9}$

8. $\frac{81}{7}$

9. $\frac{100}{8}$

Changing Mixed Numbers into Improper Fractions

It's easier to multiply and divide improper fractions than mixed numbers. You can easily change a mixed number into an improper fraction.

Example

$2\frac{3}{4}$

1. Multiply the whole number (2) by the denominator (4): $2 \times 4 = 8$

2. Add the product (8) to the numerator (3): $8 + 3 = 11$

3. Put the total (11) over the denominator (4): $\frac{11}{4}$

4. Check: Reverse the process by changing the improper fraction into a mixed number. If you get back the number you started with, your answer is right.

Practice

Convert each mixed number to an improper fraction.

10. $5\frac{4}{5}$

11. $4\frac{2}{7}$

12. $1\frac{3}{10}$

13. $10\frac{7}{8}$

14. $3\frac{5}{12}$

HERE'S A TIP

When the numerator and denominator both end in zeros, cross out the same number of zeros in both numbers to begin the reducing process. For example, $\frac{300}{4,000}$ reduces to $\frac{3}{40}$ when you cross out two zeros in both numbers.

Whenever you do arithmetic with fractions, reduce your answer. On a multiple-choice law enforcement exam, don't panic if your answer isn't listed. Try to reduce it and then compare it to the choices.

Reducing Fractions

Reducing a fraction means writing it in lowest terms, that is, with smaller numbers. For example, 50¢ is $\frac{50}{100}$ of a dollar, or $\frac{1}{2}$ of a dollar. In fact, if you have a 50¢ piece in your pocket, you say that you have a half dollar. Reducing a fraction does not change its value.

Follow these four steps to reduce a fraction:

1. Find a whole number that divides evenly into both numbers that make up the fraction.
2. Divide that number into the top of the fraction, and replace the top of the fraction with the quotient (the answer you got when you divided).
3. Do the same thing to the bottom number.
4. Repeat the first three steps until you can't find a number that divides evenly into both numbers of the fraction.

Example
Reduce $\frac{8}{24}$.
You could do it in two steps: $\frac{8 \div 4}{24 \div 4} = \frac{2}{6}$; then $\frac{2 \div 2}{6 \div 2} = \frac{1}{3}$. Or you could do it in a single step if you can find the greatest common factor: $\frac{8 \div 8}{24 \div 8} = \frac{1}{3}$.

Practice

Reduce the following fractions.

15. $\frac{10}{16}$

16. $\frac{12}{20}$

17. $\frac{24}{27}$

18. $\frac{30}{48}$

19. $\frac{56}{72}$

20. $\frac{10}{10}$

21. $\frac{40}{8,000}$

22. $\frac{200}{5,000}$

23. $\frac{30}{70}$

24. $\frac{10,000}{500,000}$

Raising Fractions to Higher Terms

Before you can add and subtract fractions, you have to know how to raise a fraction to higher terms. This is actually the opposite of reducing a fraction. To raise a fraction to higher terms:

1. Divide the original denominator into the new denominator.
2. Multiply the quotient (the step 1 answer) by the original numerator.
3. Write the product (the step 2 answer) over the new denominator.

Example

Raise $\frac{2}{3}$ to 24ths.

1. Divide the old bottom number (3) into the new one (24): $3\overline{)24} = 8$
2. Multiply the answer (8) by the old top number (2): $2 \times 8 = 16$
3. Put the answer (16) over the new bottom number (24): $\frac{16}{24}$
4. Check your answer by reducing the new fraction to see if you get back the original one: $16 \div \frac{8}{24} \div 8 = \frac{2}{3}$

Practice

For each question, raise these fractions to higher terms as indicated.

25. $\frac{1}{5} = \frac{}{20}$

26. $\frac{2}{6} = \frac{}{12}$

27. $\frac{20}{40} = \frac{}{80}$

28. $\frac{15}{25} = \frac{}{100}$

29. $\frac{50}{100} = \frac{}{1,000}$

Adding Fractions

It's important to remember that when adding or subtracting fractions, you always need them to have the same denominator. Then, whenever you subtract or add, you only need to perform the operation on the numerators, and keep the same denominator.

If the fractions have the same denominators, add the numerators together and write the total over the denominator.

Example

$\frac{2}{9} + \frac{4}{9} = \frac{2+4}{9} = \frac{6}{9}$

1. Reduce the sum: $\frac{2}{3}$

Example

Solve $\frac{5}{8} + \frac{7}{8}$. Show your answer as a mixed number and make sure it is reduced.

1. Add the numerators together: $\frac{12}{8}$
2. Change $\frac{12}{8}$ to a mixed number: $1\frac{4}{8}$
3. Reduce $1\frac{4}{8}$ to lowest terms: $1\frac{1}{2}$

There are a few extra steps to add mixed numbers with the same denominators.

Example

$2\frac{3}{5} + 1\frac{4}{5}$

1. Add the fractions: $\frac{3}{5} + \frac{4}{5} = \frac{7}{5}$
2. Change the improper fraction into a mixed number: $\frac{7}{5} = 1\frac{2}{5}$
3. Add the whole numbers: $2 + 1 = 3$
4. Add the results of steps 2 and 3: $1\frac{2}{5} + 3 = 4\frac{2}{5}$

Practice

For each question, find the sum in simplest form.

30. $\frac{1}{4} + \frac{1}{4} =$

31. $\frac{2}{10} + \frac{6}{10} =$

32. $\frac{9}{16} + \frac{2}{16} + \frac{1}{16} =$

Finding a Common Denominator

If the fractions you want to add don't have the same bottom number, you'll have to raise some or all of the fractions to higher terms so that they all have the same bottom number, a **common denominator.**

See if all the bottom numbers divide evenly into the biggest bottom number. If this fails, check out the multiplication table of the largest bottom number until you find a number that all the other bottom numbers evenly divide into. When all else fails, multiply all the bottom numbers together.

Example
$\frac{2}{3} + \frac{4}{5} =$

1. Find the common denominator. Multiply the bottom numbers: $3 \times 5 = 15$
2. Raise each fraction to 15ths: $\frac{2}{3} = \frac{2 \times 5}{3 \times 5} = \frac{10}{15}$
   $\frac{4}{5} = \frac{4 \times 3}{5 \times 3} = \frac{12}{15}$
3. Add as usual: $\frac{10}{15} + \frac{12}{15} = \frac{22}{15}$

Practice

For each question, find a common denominator.

33. $\frac{3}{4} + \frac{1}{5} =$

34. $\frac{2}{5} + \frac{5}{6} =$

35. $\frac{2}{3} + \frac{3}{4} =$

36. $\frac{7}{8} + \frac{5}{9} =$

37. $\frac{1}{2} + \frac{2}{5} =$

38. $\frac{5}{10} + \frac{6}{12} =$

Finding the Least Common Denominator

If you are asked to find the **least common denominator** (LCD), you will need to find the smallest number that is a multiple of the original denominators. Sometimes you can figure this out mentally, or you will stumble onto the LCD by following the previous steps.

However, to be sure that you have the least common denominator, you can use one of two methods:

1. Find the least common multiple. This can be done by checking out the multiplication table of the largest bottom number until you find the first number that all the other bottom numbers evenly divide into, as described previously.
2. Determine the prime factorization of each of the denominators. The least common denominator will encompass every denominator's prime factorization.

Prime numbers are numbers that have only two factors, the number 1 and itself. For example, 3 is prime because its only factors are 1 and 3. Numbers that are not prime can be expressed in terms of prime factors.

Example
$12 = 3 \times 4 = 3 \times 2 \times 2$

The prime factorization of 12 is $3 \times 2 \times 2$.

Example

Find the LCD of $\frac{3}{4}$ and $\frac{5}{6}$.

In order to find the LCD of $\frac{3}{4}$ and $\frac{5}{6}$, you can use the prime factorization method as follows:

1. Find the prime factorization of both denominators:

   $4 = 2 \times 2$

   $6 = 2 \times 3$

2. The LCD will contain the prime factorization of both denominators:

   $4 = 2 \times 2$ (the LCD must have two 2s)

   $6 = 2 \times 3$ (the LCD must have a 2 and a 3)

The LCD will be $2 \times 2 \times 3$. Note that this LCD contains the prime factorization of 4 and 6.

Practice

For each question, find the least common denominator.

39. $\frac{3}{4}$ *and* $\frac{5}{9}$

40. $\frac{3}{5}$ *and* $\frac{5}{6}$

41. $\frac{2}{7}$ *and* $\frac{6}{8}$

42. $\frac{7}{10}$ *and* $\frac{5}{12}$

43. $\frac{5}{14}$ *and* $\frac{9}{15}$

Subtracting Fractions

If the fractions have the same denominators, subtract the numerators and write the difference over the denominator.

Example

$\frac{4}{9} - \frac{3}{9} = \frac{4-3}{9} = \frac{1}{9}$

If the fractions you want to subtract don't have the same denominator, you'll have to raise some or all of the fractions to higher terms so that they all have the same bottom number, or LCD. If you forgot how to find the LCD, just read the section on adding fractions with different bottom numbers.

Example

$\frac{5}{6} - \frac{3}{4} =$

1. Raise each fraction to 12ths because 12 is the LCD, the smallest number that both 6 and 4 divide into evenly:

   $\frac{5}{6} = \frac{10}{12}$

   $\frac{3}{4} = \frac{9}{12}$

2. Subtract as usual: $\frac{10}{12} - \frac{9}{12} = \frac{1}{12}$

Subtracting mixed numbers with the same bottom number is similar to adding mixed numbers.

Example

$4\frac{3}{5} - 1\frac{2}{5} =$

1. Subtract the fractions: $\frac{3}{5} - \frac{2}{5} = \frac{1}{5}$
2. Subtract the whole numbers: $4 - 1 = 3$
3. Add the results of steps 1 and 2: $\frac{1}{5} + 3 = 3\frac{1}{5}$

Sometimes, there is an extra borrowing step when you subtract mixed numbers with the same bottom numbers.

Example

$7\frac{3}{5} - 2\frac{4}{5} =$

1. You can't subtract the fractions the way they are because $\frac{4}{5}$ is bigger than $\frac{3}{5}$. So you borrow 1 from the 7, making it 6, and change that 1 to $\frac{5}{5}$ because 5 is the bottom number: $7\frac{3}{5} = 6\frac{5}{5} + \frac{3}{5}$
2. Add the numbers from step 1: $6\frac{5}{5} + \frac{3}{5} = 6\frac{8}{5}$

3. Now you have a different version of the original problem: $6\frac{8}{5} - 2\frac{4}{5}$

4. Subtract the fractional parts of the two mixed numbers: $\frac{8}{5} - \frac{4}{5} = \frac{4}{5}$

5. Subtract the whole number parts of the two mixed numbers: $6 - 2 = 4$

6. Add the results of the last two steps together: $4 + \frac{4}{5} = 4\frac{4}{5}$

Practice

For each question, find the difference in simplest form.

44. $\frac{7}{9} - \frac{4}{9} =$

45. $\frac{11}{14} - \frac{5}{14} =$

46. $\frac{13}{15} - \frac{2}{15} - \frac{4}{15} =$

47. $\frac{5}{7} - \frac{4}{9} =$

48. $\frac{15}{16} - \frac{1}{3} - \frac{1}{6} =$

Multiplying Fractions

Multiplying fractions is actually easier than adding them. All you do is multiply the numerators and then multiply the denominators.

Example

$\frac{2}{3} \times \frac{5}{7} = \frac{2 \times 5}{3 \times 7} = \frac{10}{21}$

Sometimes, you can cancel before multiplying. Canceling is a shortcut that makes the multiplication go faster because you're multiplying with smaller numbers. It's very similar to reducing: If there is a number that divides evenly into a top number and bottom number, do that division before multiplying. If you forget to cancel, you'll still get the right answer, but you'll have to reduce it.

Example

$\frac{5}{6} \times \frac{9}{20} =$

1. Cancel the 6 and the 9 by dividing 3 into both of them: $6 \div 3 = 2$ and $9 \div 3 = 3$. Change the 6 to a 2 and the 9 to a 3:

$$\frac{5}{\overset{}{\underset{2}{\cancel{6}}}} \times \frac{\overset{3}{\cancel{9}}}{20}$$

2. Cancel the 5 and the 20 by dividing 5 into both of them: $5 \div 5 = 1$ and $20 \div 5 = 4$. Change the 5 to a 1 and the 20 to a 4:

$$\frac{\overset{1}{\cancel{5}}}{2} \times \frac{3}{\underset{4}{\cancel{20}}}$$

3. Multiply across the new top numbers and the new bottom numbers: $\frac{1 \times 3}{2 \times 4} = \frac{3}{8}$

To multiply a fraction by a whole number, first rewrite the whole number as a fraction with a bottom number of 1:

Example

$5 \times \frac{2}{3} = \frac{5}{1} \times \frac{2}{3} = \frac{5 \times 2}{1 \times 3} = \frac{10}{3}$
(Optional: convert $\frac{10}{3}$ to a mixed number: $3\frac{1}{3}$)

To multiply with mixed numbers, it's easier to change them to improper fractions before multiplying.

Example

$4\frac{2}{3} \times 5\frac{1}{2}$

1. Convert $4\frac{2}{3}$ to an improper fraction: $4\frac{2}{3} = \frac{4 \times 3 + 2}{3} = \frac{14}{3}$

2. Convert $5\frac{1}{2}$ to an improper fraction: $5\frac{1}{2} = \frac{5 \times 2 + 1}{2} = \frac{11}{2}$

3. Cancel and multiply the fractions: $\frac{14}{3} \times \frac{11}{2} = \frac{77}{3}$

4. Optional: convert the improper fraction to a mixed number: $\frac{77}{3} = 25\frac{2}{3}$

Practice

For each question, find the product in its simplest form.

49. $\frac{1}{2} \times \frac{7}{12} =$

50. $\frac{3}{4} \times \frac{6}{8} =$

51. $\frac{7}{10} \times \frac{6}{7} =$

52. $\frac{9}{16} \times \frac{12}{18} =$

53. $\frac{8}{13} \times \frac{5}{8} \times \frac{1}{5} =$

Dividing Fractions

To divide one fraction by a second fraction, invert the second fraction (that is, flip the top and bottom numbers) and then multiply.

Example

$\frac{1}{2} \div \frac{3}{5} =$

1. Invert the second fraction ($\frac{3}{5}$):
    $\frac{5}{3}$
2. Change the division sign ($\div$) to a multiplication sign ($\times$ or $\cdot$) and multiply the first fraction by the new second fraction:
    $\frac{1}{2} \times \frac{5}{3} = \frac{1 \times 5}{2 \times 3} = \frac{5}{6}$

To divide a fraction by a whole number, first change the whole number to a fraction by putting it over 1. Then follow the division steps above.

Example

$\frac{3}{5} \div 2 = \frac{3}{5} \div \frac{2}{1} = \frac{3}{5} \times \frac{1}{2} = \frac{3 \times 1}{5 \times 2} = \frac{3}{10}$

When the division problem has a mixed number, convert it to an improper fraction and then divide as usual.

Example

$2\frac{3}{4} \div \frac{1}{6} =$

1. Convert $2\frac{3}{4}$ to an improper fraction:
    $2\frac{3}{4} = 2 \times 4 + \frac{3}{4} = \frac{11}{4}$
2. Invert the second fraction ($\frac{1}{6}$):
    $\frac{6}{1}$
3. Change the division sign ($\div$) to a multiplication sign ($\times$ or $\cdot$) and multiply the new first fraction by the new second fraction:
    $\frac{11}{4} \times \frac{6}{1} = \frac{66}{4}$
4. Reduce your answer to its simplest form:
    $\frac{66}{4} = \frac{33}{2}$

Practice

For each question, find the quotient and reduce it to its simplest form.

54. $\frac{12}{17} \div \frac{3}{17} =$

55. $\frac{2}{11} \div \frac{5}{11} =$

56. $\frac{1}{6} \div \frac{5}{8} =$

57. $\frac{48}{18} \div \frac{18}{3} =$

58. $\frac{20}{36} \div \frac{20}{27} =$

Answers

1. Improper
2. Proper
3. Improper
4. Mixed
5. $7\frac{1}{2}$
6. $3\frac{2}{3}$
7. $5\frac{5}{9}$
8. $11\frac{4}{7}$
9. $12\frac{1}{2}$
10. $\frac{29}{5}$
11. $\frac{30}{7}$
12. $\frac{13}{10}$
13. $\frac{87}{8}$
14. $\frac{41}{12}$
15. $\frac{5}{8}$
16. $\frac{3}{5}$
17. $\frac{8}{9}$
18. $\frac{5}{8}$
19. $\frac{7}{9}$
20. 1
21. $\frac{1}{200}$
22. $\frac{1}{25}$
23. $\frac{3}{7}$
24. $\frac{1}{50}$
25. $x = 4$
26. $x = 4$
27. $x = 40$
28. $x = 60$
29. $x = 500$
30. $\frac{1}{2}$
31. $\frac{4}{5}$
32. $\frac{3}{4}$
33. 20
34. 30
35. 12
36. 72
37. 10
38. 120 or 60
39. 12
40. 45
41. 56
42. 60
43. 210
44. $\frac{1}{3}$
45. $\frac{3}{7}$
46. $\frac{7}{15}$
47. $\frac{17}{63}$
48. $\frac{7}{16}$
49. $\frac{7}{24}$
50. $\frac{9}{16}$
51. $\frac{3}{5}$
52. $\frac{3}{8}$
53. $\frac{1}{13}$
54. 4
55. $\frac{2}{5}$
56. $\frac{4}{15}$
57. $\frac{4}{9}$
58. $\frac{3}{4}$

 ▶ Decimals

This chapter covers decimals and different operations, as well as how to convert between fractions and decimals.

A decimal is a special kind of fraction. You use decimals every day when you deal with money—for example, $10.35 is a decimal that represents 10 dollars and 35 cents. The decimal point separates the dollars from the cents. Because there are 100 cents in one dollar, 1¢ is $\frac{1}{100}$ of a dollar, or $0.01.

Each decimal digit to the right of the decimal point has a name:

$0.1 = 1$ tenth $= \frac{1}{10}$

$0.02 = 2$ hundredths $= \frac{2}{100}$

$0.003 = 3$ thousandths $= \frac{3}{1,000}$

$0.0004 = 4$ ten-thousandths $= \frac{4}{10,000}$

When you add zeros after the rightmost number, you don't change the value of the decimal. For example, 6.17 is the same as:

6.170
6.1700
6.17000000000000000

The most important thing to remember about decimals is that the first place value to the right of the decimal point is the tenths place. The place values are as follows:

1	2	6	8	•	3	4	5	7
THOUSANDS	HUNDREDS	TENS	ONES	DECIMAL POINT	TENTHS	HUNDREDTHS	THOUSANDTHS	TEN THOUSANDTHS

In expanded form, this number can also be expressed as:

$$1{,}268.3457 = (1 \times 1{,}000) + (2 \times 100) + (6 \times 10) + (8 \times 1) + (3 \times .1) + (4 \times .01) + (5 \times .001) + (7 \times .0001)$$

Practice

Round to the nearest tenth.

1. 0.67

2. 9.009

3. 17.55

Round to the nearest hundredth.

4. 874.561

5. 0.005

6. 99.12345

Round to the nearest thousandth.

7. 560.5454

8. 1,451.8765

9. 9.9999

Changing Fractions to Decimals

To change a fraction to a decimal, divide the bottom number into the top number. You may need to put a decimal point and a few zeros on the right side of the top number. When you divide, bring the decimal point up into your answer.

Example

Change $\frac{3}{4}$ to a decimal.

Divide the bottom number (4) into 3. You will need to add two zeros to 3 and be sure to bring the decimal point up into the answer:

$$\begin{array}{r} .75 \\ 4\overline{)3.00} \\ \underline{28} \\ 20 \\ \underline{20} \\ 0 \end{array}$$

The quotient (result of the division) is the answer: 0.75.

Some fractions may require you to add many decimal zeros. In fact, when you convert a fraction like $\frac{2}{3}$ to a decimal, you can keep adding decimal zeros to the top number forever because the division will never come out evenly. As you divide 3 into 2, you'll get 6 after 6 after 6, into infinity:

$$2 \div 3 = 0.6666666666\ldots$$

This is called a repeating decimal and it can be written as $0.6\overline{66}$. You can approximate it as 0.67, 0.667, 0.6667, and so on.

Practice

Write each fraction as a decimal.

10. $\frac{3}{12}$

11. $\frac{5}{8}$

12. $\frac{9}{16}$

13. $\frac{2}{100}$

14. $\frac{761}{1,000}$

Changing Decimals to Fractions

To change a decimal to a fraction, write the digits of the decimal as the top number of a fraction, and write the decimal's name as the bottom number of the fraction. Then reduce the fraction, if possible.

Example

0.018

1. Write 18 as the top of the fraction: $\frac{18}{}$
2. Three places to the right of the decimal point means thousandths, so write 1,000 as the bottom number: $\frac{18}{1,000}$
3. Reduce the top and bottom numbers by dividing by 2: $\frac{18 \div 2}{1,000 \div 2} = \frac{9}{500}$

Practice

Write each decimal as a fraction or mixed number in simplest form.

15. 0.33

16. 0.2

17. 0.655

18. 4.07

19. 19.375

Comparing Decimals

Because decimals are easier to compare when they have the same number of digits after the decimal point, tack zeros onto the end of the shorter decimals. Then all you have to do is compare the numbers as if the decimal points weren't there:

Example
Compare 0.08 and 0.1

1. Tack one zero at the end of 0.1 to get 0.10.
2. To compare 0.10 to 0.08, just compare 10 to 8.
3. Because 10 is larger than 8, 0.1 is larger than 0.08.

Practice

Choose the larger number.

20. 6.231 or 6.321

21. 16.5 or 9.55

22. 512.338 or 512.38

23. 0.8032 or 1.08

24. 11.43781 or 11.43718

25. 0.00051 or 0.0005

Adding and Subtracting Decimals

To add or subtract decimals, line them up so their decimal points are even. You may want to tack on zeros at the end of shorter decimals so you can keep all your digits lined up evenly. Remember, if a number doesn't have a decimal point, then put one at the right end of the number.

Examples
$1.23 + 57 + 0.038 =$

1. Line up the numbers like this: 1.230
   57.000
   + 0.038
2. Add the columns: 58.268
   $1.23 - 0.038 =$
3. Add a zero to 1.23 and line up the numbers by decimal point: 1.230
   − 0.038
4. Subtract the bottom number in each column from the top: 1.192

Practice

Add the following decimals.

26. $85.6 + 0.66 =$

27. $108.47 + 8.4 =$

28. $7.91 + 6,327.7 =$

29. $19.159 + 207.44 =$

30. $62.3906 + 58.906 =$

Subtract the following decimals.

31. $7.34 - 6.2 =$

32. $38.766 - 9.558 =$

33. $144.323 - 112.705 =$

34. $89.0063 - 36.7223 =$

Multiplying Decimals

Multiplication of decimals is exactly the same as multiplication of integers, except one must make note of the total number of decimal places in the factors.

Example

What is the product of 0.14 and 4.3?

1. First, multiply as usual:

    $$\begin{array}{r} 4.3 \\ \times .14 \\ \hline 172 \\ 430 \\ \hline 602 \end{array}$$

2. Now, to figure out the answer, 4.3 has one decimal place and .14 has two decimal places. Add in order to determine the total number of decimal places the answer must have to the right of the decimal point:

    $1 + 2 = 3$ decimal places

3. When finished multiplying, start from the right side of the answer, and move to the left the number of decimal places previously calculated:

    $6 \quad 0 \quad 2$

    In this example, 602 turns into .602 since there have to be 3 decimal places in the answer.

If there are not enough digits in the answer, add in zeros in front of the answer until there are enough.

Example

Solve 0.03×0.2.

1. First, multiply:

    $$\begin{array}{r} .03 \\ \times .2 \\ \hline 6 \end{array}$$

2. There are three total decimal places in the problem; therefore, the answer must contain three decimal places. Starting to the right of 6, move left three places. The answer becomes 0.006.

Practice

Multiply the decimals that follow.

35. $4.4 \times 1.3 =$

36. $61.8 \times 1.22 =$

37. $107.4 \times 0.631 =$

38. $7.461 \times 1.55 =$

Dividing Decimals

Dividing decimals is a little different from integers for the set-up, and then regular rules of division apply. It is easier to divide if the divisor does not have any decimals. In order to accomplish that, simply move the decimal place to the right as many places as necessary to make the divisor a whole number. If the decimal point is moved in the divisor, it must also be moved in the dividend in order to keep the answer the same as the original problem. $4 \div 2$ has the same solution as its multiples $8 \div 4$ and $28 \div 14$, etc. Moving a decimal point in a division problem is equivalent to multiplying a numerator and denominator of a fraction by the same quantity, which is the reason the answer will remain the same.

If there are not enough decimal places in the answer to accommodate the required move, simply add zeros until the desired placement is achieved. Add zeros after the decimal point to continue the division until the decimal terminates, or until a repeating pattern is recognized. The decimal point in the quotient belongs directly above the decimal point in the dividend.

Example

What is $.425\overline{)1.53}$?

1. First, to make .425 a whole number, move the decimal point 3 places to the right:
425
2. Now move the decimal point 3 places to the right for 1.53:
1,530

3. The problem is now a simple long division problem:

$$
\begin{array}{r}
3.6 \\
425\overline{)1530.0} \\
-1275 \downarrow \\
\hline
2550 \\
-2550 \\
\hline
0
\end{array}
$$

Practice

Divide the decimals. If necessary, round your answer to the nearest ten thousandth.

39. $18.56 \div 8 =$

40. $213.43 \div 7 =$

41. $82.96 \div 25 =$

42. $3.57 \div 12 =$

43. $9.42 \div 6 =$

44. $123.95 \div 9 =$

Answers

1. 0.70, or 0.7

2. 9.000, or 9

3. 17.60, or 17.6

4. 874.560, or 874.56

5. 0.01

6. 99.12000, or 99.12

7. 560.5450, or 560.545

8. 1,451.8770, or 1,451.877

9. 10.0000, or 10

10. 0.25

11. 0.625

12. 0.5625

13. 0.02

14. 0.761

15. 0.33 is thirty-three hundredths, or $\frac{33}{100}$.

16. 0.2 is two tenths, or $\frac{2}{10}$. The greatest common factor of 2 and 10 is 2, so both the numerator and denominator of $\frac{2}{10}$ can be divided by 2. $\frac{2}{10} = \frac{1}{5}$.

17. 0.655 is six hundred fifty-five thousandths, or $\frac{655}{1,000}$. The greatest common factor of 655 and 1,000 is 5, so both the numerator and denominator of $\frac{655}{1,000}$ can be divided by 5. $\frac{655}{1,000} = \frac{131}{200}$.

18. 4.07 is four and seven hundredths, or $4\frac{7}{100}$.

19. 19.375 is nineteen and three hundred seventy-five thousandths, or $19\frac{375}{1,000}$. The greatest common factor of 375 and 1,000 is 125, so both the numerator and denominator of $\frac{375}{1,000}$ can be divided by 125: $\frac{375}{1,000} = \frac{3}{8}$. $19.375 = 19\frac{3}{8}$.

20. 6.321 is greater than 6.231.

21. 16.5 is greater than 9.55.

22. 512.38 is greater than 512.338.

23. 1.08 is greater than 0.8032.

24. 11.43781 is greater than 11.43718.

25. 0.00051 is greater than 0.0005.

26. 86.26

27. 116.87

28. 6,335.61

29. 226.599

30. 121.2966

31. 1.14

32. 29.208

33. 31.618

34. 52.2840, or 52.284

35. 5.72

36. 75.396

37. 67.7694

38. 11.56455

39. 2.32

40. 30.49

41. 3.3184

42. 0.2975

43. 1.57

44. 13.7722.

CHAPTER

7 ▶ Ratios, Proportions, and Percents

This chapter explains ratios and proportions and how to best work with them. It also examines the basics of percents and their relationships with fractions and decimals.

Ratios are a way of comparing numbers and they can be expressed in several ways:

- using **"to"** (3 **to** 5)
- using **"out of"** (3 **out of** 5)
- using a **colon** (3:5)
- as a **fraction** (3/5)
- as a **decimal** (0.6)

Example

Suppose your team has five plain-clothed police officers for every ten uniformed police officers. Express this information as a ratio in five different ways.

1. There is a five **to** ten ratio of plain-clothed to uniformed police officers.
2. There is a five **out of** ten ratio of plain-clothed to uniformed police officers.
3. 5:10
4. 5/10
5. 0.5

Practice

Write the following ratios as fractions.

1. 12 wins to 15 losses

2. 15 surveillance cars to 20 patrol cars

3. 5 umbrellas for 10 people

4. 6 acquittals to 4 mistrials

5. two cups of sugar for every batch of cookies

Write the following ratios using a colon.

6. 5 DNA samples to 40 suspects

7. one set of fingerprints to one person

8. three people failed for every nine who passed

9. three correct answers for every incorrect answer

10. two sprints to 10 sit-ups

Proportions

A **proportion** states that two ratios are equal to each other. For example, have you ever heard someone say something like this?

Nine out of ten professional athletes suffer at least one injury each season.

The words *nine out of ten* are a ratio. They tell you that 9/10 of the professional athletes suffer at least one injury each season. But there are more than ten professional athletes. Suppose that there are 100 professional athletes. Then 9/10 of the 100 athletes, or 90 out of 100 professional athletes, suffer at least one injury per season. The two ratios are equivalent and form a proportion:

9/10 = 90/100

Here are some other proportions:

3/5 = 6/10
1/2 = 5/10
2/5 = 22/55

Notice that a proportion reflects equivalent fractions: Each fraction reduces to the same value.

As with fractions, the **cross products** of a proportion are equal.

$$\frac{3}{5} \diagup\!\!\!\!\diagdown \frac{6}{10}$$

$3 \times 10 = 5 \times 6$

Example

Are 9/12 and 18/24 a proportion?

Multiply the cross-products:

$24 \times 9 \overset{?}{=} 18 \times 12$

$216 = 216$

These fractions represent a proportion.

Practice

Solve for the missing number in each proportion. Use cross multiplication to check your answers.

11. 5/8 = ?/32

12. 2/9 = ?/810

13. 1/8 = ?/640

14. 7/10 = ?/110

15. 5/6 = ?/36

16. 3/4 = ?/120

17. 45/50 = ?/250

HERE'S A TIP

If two proportions are **directly proportional**, then one increases by a certain factor as the other increases by the same factor. If one decreases by a certain factor, the other decreases by that same factor.

   If someone has a job, the amount of money he or she earns may be directly proportional to the amount of hours worked. Maybe if he or she works twice as long, the pay is twice as much. If he or she works half the amount, the pay is half.

   Two proportions are **inversely proportional** if an increase by a certain factor for one is accompanied by a decrease by that same factor for the other.

Scale Drawings

Sometimes, you will encounter ratio questions that deal with scale drawings. **Scale drawings** are used to represent objects that are too large or too small to be drawn or built to actual size. The scale is determined by the ratio of a given length on the drawing or model to its corresponding length in real life.

Example

Suppose you are given a map with a scale of 1 inch = 90 miles. If the distance between Virginia Beach, Virginia, and New York City, New York, on the map is 4 inches, what is the actual distance?

1. The ratio is 1 inch/90 miles. Set that equal to 4 inches/x:
   1 inch/90 miles = 4 inches/x
2. Cross-multiply and solve:
   $1x = (90)(4)$
   $x = 360$
   So, the actual distance is 360 miles.

Practice

Solve the following proportion problems using the information provided.

18. The ratio of traffic violations to parking offenses is 2:5. If there are 10 traffic violations, how many parking offenses are there?

19. One inch represents 0.5 mile on a map. If the police station is 3.5 inches away from your house on the map, how many miles away is the police station?

20. Samantha bought two $5 books for every $8 book.

   a. If she bought eight $5 books, how many $8 books did Samantha buy?

   b. How many books did Samantha buy in total?

   c. How much money did Samantha spend in total?

Percents

Percents are everywhere you look. Stores frequently advertise sales with signs announcing "20% off" or "Take an additional 30% off." Packages at the super-market regularly claim to include "30% more free."

   Percents are always "out of 100." 45% means 45 out of 100. You can also express 45% as:

- a decimal: 45% = 0.45
- a fraction: 45% = 45/100

Converting Percents to Decimals

Changing percents to decimals is as simple as moving the decimal point two digits to the left. Here are the basic steps.

Step 1 Drop the percent sign.

Step 2 Add a decimal point if there isn't already one. Remember that even when it's not written, whole numbers are followed by a decimal point.

Step 3 Move the decimal point two places to the left.

Example

Convert 25% to a decimal.

1. Drop the percent sign. So, 25% becomes 25.
2. Add a decimal point:
   25.
3. Move the decimal point two places to the left:
   0.25
   So, 25% = 0.25

Example

Convert 22.5% to a decimal.

1. Drop the percent sign:
   22.5
2. There is already a decimal point in place, so move the decimal point two places to the left:
   0.225
   So, 22.5% = 0.225

Practice

Convert these percents to decimals.

21. 25%

22. 12%

23. 50%

24. 62.5%

25. 4.2%

26. 0.2%

27. 125%

28. 100%

29. 128.9%

30. 2,000%

Converting Decimals to Percents

Changing decimals to percents is the opposite of what you've just done. Here are the basic steps.

Step 1. Move the decimal point two places to the right. If there aren't enough digits to move the decimal point over two places, add zeros.

Step 2. Add a percent sign after the number.

Example

Convert 0.15 to a percent.

1. Move the decimal point two places to the right. So, 0.15 becomes 15.
2. Add a percent sign after the number: 15%
   So, 0.15 = 15%.

Example

Convert 7.9 to a percent.

1. Move the decimal point two places to the right. Add zeros as needed. So, 7.9 becomes 790.
2. Add a percent sign after the number: 790%
   So, 7.9 = 790%.

Practice

Convert these decimals to percents.

31. 0.40

32. 0.75

33. 0.625

34. 0.29

35. 0.33

36. 1.56

37. 2.0

38. 6.5

39. 3.56

40. 8.0

Converting Percents to Fractions

To change a percent to a fraction, you write the percent over 100. Don't forget to reduce the fraction to lowest terms as you would any other fraction. Here are the steps to follow.

Step 1. Drop the percent sign.

Step 2. Write the number as a fraction over 100.

Step 3. Write improper fractions as mixed numbers. Reduce the fraction to lowest terms.

Example

Convert 15% to a fraction.

1. Drop the percent sign. 15% becomes 15
2. Write the number as a fraction over 100:
    $\frac{15}{100}$
3. Reduce the fraction to lowest terms. Both 15 and 100 can be divided by 5:
    $\frac{15 \div 5}{100 \div 5} = \frac{3}{20}$

    So, 15% = $\frac{3}{20}$

Example

Convert 150% to a fraction.

1. Drop the percent sign. 150% becomes 150.
2. Write the number as a fraction over 100:
    $\frac{150}{100}$
3. Write the improper fraction as a mixed number, and reduce the fraction to lowest terms:
    $\frac{150 \div 50}{100 \div 50} = \frac{3}{2} = 1\frac{1}{2}$

    So, 150% = $1\frac{1}{2}$.

What if the percent already has a fraction in it?

Example

Convert $15\frac{1}{2}$% to a fraction.

1. Drop the percent sign:
    $15\frac{1}{2}$
2. Write the number as a fraction over 100:
    $\frac{15\frac{1}{2}}{100}$
3. Remember that the bar in a fraction means to divide. So you can rewrite this problem as a division problem:
    $15\frac{1}{2} \div 100$

4. Change the mixed number $15\frac{1}{2}$ to an improper fraction:
    $\frac{31}{2} \div 100$
5. Invert the second fraction and multiply:
    $\frac{31}{2} \times \frac{1}{100} = \frac{31}{200}$
    Because the fraction is already in simplest form, you're done. So, $15\frac{1}{2}$% = $\frac{31}{200}$.

Practice

Convert these percents to fractions in simplest form.

41. 16%

42. 5%

43. 25%

44. 80%

45. 34%

46. 10%

47. 89%

48. 3%

49. $87\frac{1}{2}$%

50. $16\frac{2}{3}$ %

Converting Fractions to Percents

There are two basic ways to convert fractions to percents. You should try both ways, and see which one works best for you.

Method 1

Step 1. Divide the numerator by the denominator.

Step 2. Multiply by 100. (This is the same as moving the decimal point two digits to the right.)

Step 3. Add a percent sign.

Method 2

Step 1. Multiply the fraction by $\frac{100}{1}$.

Step 2. Write the product as either a whole or a mixed number.

Step 3. Add a percent sign.

Example

Change $\frac{2}{5}$ to a percent.

Method 1

1. Divide the numerator by the denominator:

$$5\overline{)2.0} \quad \begin{array}{c} 0.4 \\ \underline{20} \end{array}$$

2. Multiply the product by 100:

   $0.4 \times 100 = 40$

3. Add a percent sign:

   40%

Method 2

1. Multiply the fraction by $\frac{100}{1}$

   $\frac{2}{5} \times \frac{100}{1} = \frac{200}{5} = \frac{40}{1}$

2. Write the product as either a whole or a mixed number:

   40

3. Add a percent sign:

   40%

To convert a mixed number to a percent, first change it to an improper fraction. Then, follow either Method 1 or Method 2 shown previously.

Example

Convert $2\frac{1}{2}$ to a percent.

1. Change the mixed number to an improper fraction:

   $2\frac{1}{2} = \frac{5}{2}$

2. Multiply the fraction by $\frac{100}{1}$:

   $\frac{5}{2} \times \frac{100}{1} = \frac{500}{2} = \frac{250}{1}$

3. Write the product as either a whole or a mixed number.

   250

4. Add a percent sign:

   250%

So, $2\frac{1}{2} = 250\%$.

Practice

Convert these fractions to percents.

51. $\frac{3}{4}$

52. $\frac{1}{2}$

53. $\frac{3}{5}$

54. $\frac{1}{4}$

55. $\frac{3}{50}$

56. $\frac{1}{8}$

57. $\frac{7}{10}$

58. $\frac{17}{20}$

59. $\frac{19}{25}$

60. $\frac{18}{5}$

61. $3\frac{1}{4}$

62. $9\frac{4}{5}$

HERE'S A TIP

Although you can always convert between percents, decimals, and fractions using the described methods, it's a good idea to know common percent, decimal, and fraction equivalents for standardized tests. Knowing them in advance can save you valuable time on a timed test. Besides, working with a value in one form is often easier than working with it in another form. Knowing the equivalents can help you see the easier route faster. Here are some common equivalents you might want to learn.

EQUIVALENTS TO KNOW

PERCENT	DECIMAL	FRACTION
1%	0.01	$\frac{1}{100}$
5%	0.05	$\frac{5}{100}$
10%	0.1	$\frac{1}{10}$
12.5%	0.125	$\frac{1}{8}$
20%	0.2	$\frac{1}{5}$
25%	0.25	$\frac{1}{4}$
$33\frac{1}{3}$%	$0.\overline{3}$	$\frac{1}{3}$
40%	0.40	$\frac{2}{5}$
50%	0.5	$\frac{1}{2}$
$66\frac{2}{3}$%	$0.\overline{6}$	$\frac{2}{3}$
75%	0.75	$\frac{3}{4}$
80%	0.80	$\frac{4}{5}$
90%	0.90	$\frac{9}{10}$
100%	1.0	$\frac{1}{1} = 1$

Practice

Complete the question without a calculator.

63. Fill in the second column below with the decimal and fraction equivalents to the given percent. More than one response may be correct. The first has been completed for you as a guide.

When I see...	I will write...
25%	$\frac{1}{4}$ and 0.25
32%	_____
80%	_____
95%	_____
150%	_____
500%	_____

Solving Percent Problems

Percent problems ask you to find one of three things: the part, the whole, or the percent. Here's how these three elements are related to one another.

Whole × Percent = Part

This is called an *equation*, or a kind of math sentence. It tells how different elements are related to one another. You can use this equation to find any one of the elements that might be missing.

Finding a Part of a Whole

Often you will be asked to find a part of a whole. In these problems, you are given a whole and a percent, and are asked to find the part represented by the percent of the whole.

Example

What is 30% of 60?

1. Begin by figuring out what you know from the problem and what you're looking for.
   You have the percent: 30%.
   You have the whole: 60.
   You are looking for the part.
2. Then, use the equation to solve the problem:
   Whole × Percent = Part
   Plug in the pieces of the equation that you know: 60 × 30% = Part
3. Convert the percent to a decimal to make your multiplication easier: 60 × 0.30 = Part
4. Solve: 60 × 0.30 = 18.

So, 30% of 60 is 18.

Example

Only 10% of the test takers did not pass the police officer exam. There are 20 test takers. How many test takers did not pass the police officer exam?

1. Begin by figuring out what you know from the problem and what you're looking for.
   You have the percent: 10%.
   You have the whole: 20 test takers.
   You are looking for the part—the number of test takers who did not pass the police officer exam.
2. Then, use the equation to solve the problem: Whole × Percent = Part
   Plug in the pieces of the equation that you know: 20 × 10% = Part

3. Convert the percent to a decimal to make your multiplication easier: 20 × 0.10 = Part
4. Solve: 20 × 0.10 = 2.

So, two test takers did not pass the police officer exam.

Practice

Solve each problem.

64. What is 1% of 34?

65. What is 10% of 52?

66. What is 0.5% of 30?

67. What is 100% of 99?

68. What is 25% of 100?

69. What is 20% of 70?

70. What is 90% of 10?

71. What is 80% of 50?

Finding a Percent

In the following types of problems, you will be given the part and the whole. Your task is to determine what percent the part is of the whole. Remember that a percent is just a fraction written over 100. You can solve these types of problems by writing the part over the whole and converting the fraction to a percent.

Example

10 is what percent of 200?

1. Begin by figuring out what you know from the problem and what you're looking for.
   You have the part: 10.
   You have the whole: 200.
   You are looking for the percent.
2. Write a fraction of the part over the whole:
   $\frac{10}{200}$
3. Convert the fraction to a percent. Remember there are two methods for converting fractions to percents. Use either method. Method 1 is shown below:
   $10 \div 200 = 0.05$
   $0.05 \times 100 = 5$
   5%

So, 10 is 5% of 200.

Example

There are 500 people in the police academy graduating class. Fifty people in the class are graduating with honors. What percent of the class is graduating with honors?

1. Begin by figuring out what you know from the problem and what you're looking for.
   You have the part: 50.
   You have the whole: 500.
   You are looking for the percent.
2. Write a fraction of the part over the whole:
   $\frac{50}{500}$
3. Convert the fraction to a percent. Remember there are two methods for converting fractions to percents. Use either method. Method 1 is shown below:
   $50 \div 500 = 0.1$
   $0.1 \times 100 = 10$
   10%

So, 10% of the class is graduating with honors.

HERE'S A TIP

Sometimes, this type of problem will ask you to find a percent change. The problem will give you one part of the whole. Your task is to calculate the part of the whole represented by the *difference* between the whole and the part given. When you see these types of phrases, you are probably being asked to calculate the part of the whole represented by the *difference* between the whole and the part given:

- Find the percent change.
- Find the percent increase.
- Find the percent decrease.
- By what percent did it improve?
- By what percent did it go down?
- By what percent did it go up?

Practice

Solve each problem.

72. 10 is what percent of 50?

73. 20 is what percent of 80?

74. 5 is what percent of 20?

75. 6 is what percent of 6?

76. 9 is what percent of 18?

77. 1 is what percent of 50?

78. 22 is what percent of 100?

Finding the Whole

In the following types of problems, you will be given the part and the percent. Your task is to determine the whole. You can solve these types of problems by writing the part over the percent and dividing.

$$\text{Whole} = \frac{\text{Part}}{\text{Percent}}$$

Example

45 is 75% percent of what number?

1. Begin by figuring out what you know from the problem and what you're looking for.
   You have the part: 45
   You also have the percent: 75%
   You are looking for the whole.
2. Write the part over the percent:
   $\frac{45}{75\%}$
3. Convert the percent to a fraction to make your division easier: $45 \div \frac{75}{100} = \text{Whole}$
4. Solve:
   $45 \div \frac{75}{100}$
   $\frac{45}{1} \times \frac{100}{75} = 60$

So, 45 is 75% of 60.

Example

Five members of a running club qualified for the local marathon. This represents 20% of the running club. How many members are in the running club?

1. Begin by figuring out what you know from the problem and what you're looking for.
   You have the part: 5 members
   You also have the percent: 20%
   You are looking for the whole.
2. Write the part over the percent:
   $\frac{5}{20\%}$
3. Convert the percent to a fraction to make your division easier: $5 \div \frac{20}{100} = \text{Whole}$
4. Solve:
   $5 \div \frac{20}{100}$
   $\frac{5}{1} \times \frac{100}{20} = 25$

So, there are 25 members in the running club.

Practice

Solve these problems.

79. 20 is 20% of what number?

80. 30 is 75% of what number?

81. 6 is 50% of what number?

82. 75 is 75% of what number?

83. 20 is 2% of what number?

84. 40% of what number is 100?

85. 10% of what number is 5?

86. 80% of what number is 120?

87. 200% of what number is 50?

HERE'S A TIP

Instead of rearranging the percent equation for each type of problem, you can use it to set up a proportion like the one shown below.

$$\frac{\text{Part}}{\text{Whole}} = \frac{\%}{100}$$

You can use this proportion to solve all three types of percent problems. You *cross multiply* to solve each time. To cross multiply, multiply the numerator (or top number) of the first fraction by the denominator (or bottom number) of the second fraction and the denominator of the first fraction by the numerator of the second fraction. The result will look like this:

Part × 100 = Whole × %

Answers

1. 12/15, which can be reduced to 4/5
2. 15/20, which can be reduced to 3/4
3. 5/10, which can be reduced to 1/2
4. 6/4, which can be reduced to 3/2
5. 2/1
6. 5:40, which can be reduced to 1:8
7. 1:1
8. 3:9, which can be reduced to 1:3
9. 3:1
10. 2:10, which can be reduced to 1:5
11. 20

   Cross multiply to check your work:

   5 × 32 = 8 × 20

   160 = 160
12. 180

   Cross multiply to check your work:

   2 × 810 = 9 × 180

   1,620 = 1,620
13. 80

   Cross multiply to check your work:

   1 × 640 = 8 × 80

   640 = 640
14. 77

   Cross multiply to check your work:

   7 × 110 = 10 × 77

   770 = 770
15. 30

   Cross multiply to check your work:

   5 × 36 = 6 × 30

   180 = 180
16. 90

   Cross multiply to check your work:

   4 × 90 = 3 × 120

   360 = 360
17. 225

   Cross multiply to check your work:

   45 × 250 = 50 × 225

   11,250 = 11,250
18. There are 25 parking offenses.
19. The police station is 1.75 miles from home.
20. a. Samantha bought 4 $8 books.
    b. Samantha bought a total of 12 books.
    c. Samantha spent $72 in total.
21. 0.25
22. 0.12
23. 0.50 or 0.5
24. 0.625
25. 0.042
26. 0.002
27. 1.25
28. 1.00 or 1
29. 1.289
30. 20.00 or 20
31. 40%
32. 75%
33. 62.5%
34. 29%
35. 33%
36. 156%
37. 200%
38. 650%
39. 356%
40. 800%

41. $\frac{16}{100}$, which reduces to $\frac{4}{25}$

42. $\frac{5}{100}$, which reduces to $\frac{1}{20}$

43. $\frac{25}{100}$, which reduces to $\frac{1}{4}$

44. $\frac{80}{100}$, which reduces to $\frac{4}{5}$

45. $\frac{34}{100}$, which reduces to $\frac{17}{50}$

46. $\frac{10}{100}$, which reduces to $\frac{1}{10}$

47. $\frac{89}{100}$

48. $\frac{3}{100}$

49. $\frac{7}{8}$

50. $\frac{1}{6}$

51. 75%

52. 50%

53. 60%

54. 25%

55. 6%

56. 12.5%

57. 70%

58. 85%

59. 76%

60. 360%

61. 325%

62. 980%

63. See answers in bold.

When I see...	I will write...
25%	$\frac{1}{4}$ **and 0.25**
32%	**0.32,** $\frac{32}{100}$**,** $\frac{8}{25}$
80%	$\frac{80}{100}$**,** $\frac{4}{5}$**, 0.8**
95%	$\frac{95}{100}$**, 0.95**
150%	$\frac{150}{100}$**,** $\frac{3}{2}$**, 1.5**
500%	$\frac{500}{100}$**,** $\frac{5}{1}$**, 5**

64. 0.34

65. 5.2

66. 0.15

67. 99

68. 25

69. 14

70. 9

71. 40

72. 20%

73. 25%

74. 25%

75. 100%

76. 50%

77. 2%

78. 22%

79. 100

80. 40

81. 12

82. 100

83. 1,000

84. 250

85. 50

86. 150

87. 25

8 ▶ Word Problems

This chapter demonstrates some strategies for dealing with word problems.

Solving a math problem that contains only numbers is usually straightforward. You're given a couple of numbers, an operation to perform, such as addition or subtraction, and asked to find the answer. That same question, given as a word problem, can be a bit tougher.

The Keywords of Word Problems

Often, the hardest part of a word problem isn't the computation—it's figuring out what operation to use. When working with math problems, a keyword is a word that signals what operation to use. A problem might contain more than one keyword, especially if the word problem requires more than one operation to solve. There are several keywords that often signal addition, subtraction, multiplication, and division.

ADDITION	SUBTRACTION	MULTIPLICATION	DIVISION
increased by	decreased by	of	per, a
more than	minus	times, multiplied by	out of
combined	less	product of	ratio of, quotient of
together, altogether	difference between/of	increased/decreased by a factor of	percent (divide by 100)
total of	less than, fewer than		quotient
sum	difference		share
plus	minus		average
both	left		each
more	remain		

HERE'S A TIP

When working on a word problem, underline the keywords. Some word problems can be long because they either contain information not needed to solve the problem or because they require more than one operation to solve. By underlining the keywords, you can help yourself remember which operation(s) you need to solve the problem.

Practice

For each problem, underline the keywords and choose the operation needed to solve the problem. Then, find the solution to the problem.

1. Find the product of 15 and 9.

2. At a law firm, Dean has 19 more cases than Andrea. If Andrea has 33 cases, how many cases does Dean have?

3. Twenty students share 220 books evenly. How many books does each student receive?

4. The bull's eye of Matt's dartboard is worth 45 points for every time it is hit. If Matt hits the bull's eye 14 times, how many points will he score?

5. If 25 is increased by 37, what is the new value?

6. A group of 12 skiers pays $420 for lift tickets. What is the average cost of a ticket per person?

7. A store receives a shipment of 55 snow shovels. If 38 of the shovels are sold, how many remain in stock?

8. What is the quotient of 126 and 42?

9. Maurice and Steve play hockey for the Blizzard. If Maurice scored 37 goals this season, and Steve scored 24 goals this season, how many goals did they score altogether?

10. Natila brings 75 euros to France. If she spends 59 euros, how many euros does she have left?

Breaking Down Word Problems

The following steps can be used to solve a word problem.

Step 1: Read the Entire Word Problem

Some word problems can be long, so be sure to read all the information carefully. Even if a word problem is short, be sure to read carefully. If you misread the problem, you may choose the wrong operation or set your number sentence up incorrectly. How easy is it to read too fast? Check out these three examples.

Example 1
Cindy's beaker contains 273 milliliters of water and Nancy's beaker contains 237 milliliters of water. If 38 milliliters are poured from Cindy's beaker to Nancy's beaker, how much water is now in Cindy's beaker?

Example 2
Cindy's beaker contains 273 milliliters of water and Nancy's beaker contains 237 milliliters of water. If 38 milliliters are poured from Cindy's beaker to Nancy's beaker, how much water is now in Nancy's beaker?

Example 3
Cindy's beaker contains 273 milliliters of water and Nancy's beaker contains 237 milliliters of water. If 38 milliliters were poured from Cindy's beaker to Nancy's beaker, how much water was in Cindy's beaker?

These three word problems are very similar, but the answers to each are different. Did you catch the differences? The first problem asks you to find how much water is in Cindy's beaker after 38 milliliters are poured from her beaker into Nancy's beaker. Since water left Cindy's beaker, you need to subtract 38 from 273: 273 − 38 = 235 milliliters.

The second word problem also states that 38 milliliters are poured from Cindy's beaker into Nancy's beaker, but this problem wants you to find how much water is now in Nancy's beaker. Since the amount of water in Nancy's beaker increased, you need to add 38 to 237: 38 + 237 = 275 milliliters.

The third word problem again states that 38 milliliters are poured from Cindy's beaker into Nancy's beaker, but this problem tells you that 273 milliliters is the volume of water in Cindy's beaker after 38 milliliters were poured out, and the problem asks you to find out how much water was in Cindy's beaker before those 38 milliliters were poured out. You need to add 38 milliliters to the volume in Cindy's breaker now to find out how much water was in the beaker: 273 + 38 = 311 milliliters.

Two of these word problems required addition and one required subtraction, and even the two that used addition were different. That's why the first step in solving a word problem is to read the entire word problem, and read it carefully.

Step 2: Underline the Keywords

Once you have the keywords underlined, you'll either know which operation to use, or you will have limited the possible operations to just a few. What if there are no keywords in a word problem? When this happens, you must use the context of the word problem to help you limit the possible operations.

Step 3: List the Possible Operations

By making a list, you can test each operation and cross out the ones that are incorrect.

Example
Officer Lui walks 17 blocks to work. If Officer Bernhardt walks 4 fewer blocks to work, how many blocks does Officer Bernhardt walk to get to work?

1. Read the entire word problem. The problem contains the numbers 17 and 4,

and you are looking for the number of blocks Officer Bernhardt walks to get to work.

2. Underline the keywords. You should have underlined the word *fewer*, which signals subtraction.

3. List the possible operations. You already have subtraction as a possibility, but check the context of the problem. The number of blocks Officer Lui walks is given, and you are looking for the number of blocks Officer Bernhardt walks. You are told that Officer Bernhardt walks 4 fewer blocks than Officer Lui, which tells you the number of blocks Officer Bernhardt walks will be less than 17. You are looking for an operation that will make the number 17 smaller. Using division wouldn't make sense, so the only possibility is subtraction.

Step 4: Write Number Sentences for Each Operation

By writing number sentences for each operation, you can help determine which operations make sense. You can also determine if you've placed the numbers, or operands, in the correct position in the number sentence. For some operations, like addition and multiplication, the order of the operands doesn't matter, but for operations like subtraction and division, order is very important.

In the example of Officer Bernhardt and Officer Lui, you've decided to use subtraction, and the problem contains the numbers 17 and 4. There are two number sentences you can form: $17 - 4$ and $4 - 17$.

Once you have written the possible number sentences for the word problem, you're ready to produce one or more possible answers.

Step 5: Solve the Number Sentences and Decide Which Answer Is Reasonable

You came up with two possible number sentences for the example of Officer Bernhardt and Officer Lui. Let's solve each: $17 - 4 = 13$ and $4 - 17 = -3$. Which answer is reasonable? It would be impossible to walk -3 blocks to work. You know from the context of the problem that Officer Bernhardt walks fewer blocks than Officer Lui, and 13 blocks are less than 17 blocks. 13 is the reasonable answer.

Step 6: Check Your Work

Check the answer to a problem by using the inverse of the operation used to find your answer. You used subtraction to find the answer to this problem, so you will use addition to check the answer. $13 + 4 = 17$, the number of blocks Officer Lui walks. You have performed the subtraction correctly.

Example
Judah read 5 books in the month of May. The first book contains 241 pages and the second book contains 312 pages. How many pages were the first two books combined?

1. Read the entire word problem. This word problem isn't long, and you can tell that you need to use the sizes of each book to find our answer.

2. Underline the keywords. The word *combined* is a keyword that signals addition.

3. List the possible operations. Addition is the only reasonable operation. You need to find the total number of pages in the first two books, so operations that decrease a number, such as subtraction and division, won't work. Multiplying the book sizes would give you a huge number that is much greater than the number of pages in the two books.

4. Write number sentences for each operation.

241 + 312

312 + 241

5. The order of the addends in an addition sentence doesn't matter, so you can eliminate the second number sentence, since it will give you the same total as the first number sentence. What about the number 5? You are also told that Judah read 5 books in the month of May. This number cannot help you solve the problem; in fact, it might be included in the word problem just to trick us. Numbers like this are extraneous information, so cross out the number 5. Eliminating extraneous information will make writing and choosing the correct number sentence easier.

Our word problem now looks like this:

~~Judah read 5 books in the month of May.~~ The first book contains 241 pages and the second book contains 312 pages. How many pages were the first two books <u>combined</u>?

6. Solve the number sentences and decide which answer is reasonable. You only have one number sentence: 241 + 312 = 553 pages.

HERE'S A TIP

Extraneous information is anything that is given in a word problem but not needed to solve the word problem. Long descriptions, numbers that are not needed to find the answer, or background information could be extraneous information. Reading through extra text can slow you down, and extra numbers in a word problem could confuse you into writing the wrong number sentence.

7. Check your work. Use subtraction to check addition. Subtract the total number of pages from either the number of pages in the first book or the number of pages in the second book. The total minus the number of pages in the first book should give you the number of pages in the second book (and the total minus the number of pages in the second book should give you the number of pages in the first book). 553 − 241 = 312 and 553 − 312 = 241. Our answer is correct.

Practice

Solve the following word problems. Show your work using the steps described above.

11. A relay race is run by 5 athletes. If the race is 1,000 meters, and each athlete runs the same distance, how far does each athlete run?

12. A machine produces 420 products in an hour. How many products will the machine produce in 7 hours?

13. Jonathan's disc can hold 1,440 megabytes. The files on the disc right now take up 865 megabytes. How many megabytes are remaining on the disc?

14. A truck driver made 18 deliveries last week and 24 deliveries this week. How many deliveries did the driver make altogether?

15. Allie swam 55 laps every day for 15 days. How many laps did she swim over that period of time?

16. A box holds 625 index cards. If Emma uses 313 cards, how many cards are left in the box?

17. Ethan has 12 rolls of nickels. Each roll holds 40 nickels. How many nickels does Ethan have?

18. David records 1,565 minutes of footage over 5 days. How many minutes of footage did he record on average each day?

19. A polar bear loses 45 pounds over the course of a year. If the weight of the polar bear was 903 pounds at the start of the year, what is the weight of the bear at the end of the year?

20. Monica rides the subway for 35 minutes and then walks another 13 minutes to get to work. If the subway moved at an average speed of 45 miles per hour, how long did it take Monica to get to work?

21. A stamp costs 44 cents. Lisa buys 25 stamps and uses them to mail 11 packages. How much money did Lisa spend on stamps?

22. Lindsay flies 2,462 miles in 5 hours, while Jamie flies 719 miles in 2 hours. How much farther does Lindsay fly than Jamie?

23. A concert hall contains 3,450 seats. If 3,216 seats are sold for a show, and the cost is $18 per ticket, how much money did the concert hall collect?

24. Lincoln College enrolled 2,314 students last year. If the number of students increased by 239 this year, and the cost of tuition increased by $1,200, how many students are attending Lincoln College this year?

Word Problem Pitfalls

You've seen how to translate keywords into operations and how to break down a word problem. How-ever, sometimes keywords and phrases can be misleading and following are several things to watch out for.

Backward Phrases

The phrase *add 4 and 6* can be converted into the number sentence 4 + 6. The numbers fit right into the number sentence as they appear in the phrase. What about the phrase *subtract 4 from 6*? At first glance, you might want to write 4 − 6. Read the phrase again carefully: subtract 4 from 6. You are starting with 6 and taking 4. This phrase, written as a number sentence, is 6 − 4. This kind of phrase is a **backward phrase**, or a group of words and numbers that describe an operation in which the numbers are given in the opposite order that they will appear in a number sentence.

Misleading Keywords

You've learned how the word *each* could signal multiplication or division and the keyword phrases *more than* and *less than* signal subtraction every time. However, some word problems are written in such a way that these phrases actually signal addition.

Example

The town of Glenbrook received 12 inches of rain more than the town of Eastland over a six-week period. If Eastland received 14 inches of rain during that time, how many inches of rain did Glenbrook receive?

1. Read the entire word problem. You are given the amount of rainfall Eastland received and the number of inches more than Eastland that Glenbrook received. You are looking for the number of inches of rain Glenbrook received.
2. Underline the keywords. The keyword phrase *more than* usually signals subtraction. However, you're given the total rainfall for Eastland, not Glenbrook.

Since Glenbrook received more rainfall than Eastland, you will have to add the number of inches more to the number of inches Eastland received.

3. Cross out extra information and translate words into numbers. You are told that the rainfall occurred over a six-week period, but the number 6 isn't needed to solve this problem.

4. List the possible operations. Subtraction seemed like a possibility, so you will write number sentences for subtraction, but the context of the problem tells you that addition is likely the right choice.

5. Write number sentences for each operation:

   14 + 12

   14 – 12

   12 – 14

6. Solve the number sentences and decide which answer is reasonable:

   14 + 12 = 26 inches

   14 – 12 = 2 inches

   12 – 14 = –2 inches

   Glenbrook received more rain than Eastland, so our answer must be greater than 14 inches. You're looking for an operation that increases 14, so subtraction is not the operation to use. You must add to find the total rainfall in Glenbrook.

7. Check your work. You'll use subtraction to check your answer. If Glenbrook received 12 more inches than Eastland, then the number of inches Glenbrook received, 26, minus 12 should equal the number of inches Eastland received, 14: 26 – 12 = 14 inches.

Opposite Operations

A word problem can sometimes describe an action or operation that already occurred. Some problems will give you the result of an operation, and then ask you to find the original value. Think about how you check your work after performing an operation; after an addition problem, you use subtraction, and after a subtraction problem, you use addition. You always use the opposite operation to check your work, since you check your work by undoing what you did to solve the problem. If a word problem describes an operation that has already been performed, you must use the opposite of that operation to find the original value.

Example

The difference between two numbers is 34. If the smaller number is 16, what is the larger number?

1. Read the entire word problem. You are given the difference between two numbers and the smaller of the two numbers. You are looking for the larger of the two numbers.

2. Underline the keywords. The keyword **difference** usually signals subtraction, but the first sentence of this word problem tells you that the difference has already been found. Addition is the opposite of subtraction, so you must use addition to solve this problem.

3. List the possible operations. You must use addition to solve this problem.

4. Write number sentences for each operation.

   Just one number sentence: 16 + 34.

5. Solve the number sentence and decide whether the answer is reasonable.

   16 + 34 = 50

   Our answer is larger than 16, so it seems reasonable.

6. Check your work. You can check our answer by finding the difference between the two numbers. You're told in the word problem that the difference is 34: 50 – 16 = 34, so our answer is correct.

Multi-Step Problems

Some word problems take more than one operation to solve. How can you spot a word problem that requires more than one step? These problems are usually a little longer and may contain more than one keyword. If you see a keyword that signals multiplication, and then another keyword that signals subtraction, it is likely the problem will require at least two steps to solve. One of the most common types of these problems is finding change after making multiple purchases.

Example

Alana buys 3 pairs of shoes, each for $49 including tax. If she gives the cashier $150, how much change will she receive?

1. Read the entire word problem. You are given the number of pairs of shoes Alana buys, the price of one pair of shoes, and how much Alana gives the cashier. You are looking for how much change she receives.

2. Underline the keywords. The keyword *each* can signal multiplication or division, and the word *change* often signals subtraction.

3. Cross out extra information and translate words into numbers. This problem contains three numbers; you will need all three numbers to solve the problem. The number of pairs of shoes and the price of each pair are needed to determine the total price, and the amount Alana gave the cashier will be needed to find her change. There is no extra information in this problem.

4. List the possible operations. You are given the price of one pair of shoes and you are looking for the price of three pairs of shoes. When you are given the value of one and you're looking for the total value of more than one, you need to use multiplication. In order to find change, you need to subtract a total price from an amount of money paid. To solve this problem, you will need to multiply first, and then subtract.

5. Write number sentences for each operation. The total Alana must pay is equal to three times the price of one pair of shoes: $49 × 3. You can't form your subtraction sentence yet because you need the result of that multiplication sentence.

6. Solve the number sentences and decide which answer is reasonable: $49 × 3 = $147. Since the price of one pair of shoes is $49, $147 seems like a reasonable price for 3 pairs of shoes. However, this is not your answer, since you are looking for how much change Alana receives after she gives the cashier $150. You must return to the previous step and write another number sentence.

7. Write number sentences for each operation. Alana gives the cashier $150 for shoes that cost a total of $147. Her change will be equal to the difference between these two numbers: $150 − $147. This is our only number sentence; it would not make sense to subtract $150 from $147.

8. Solve the number sentences and decide which answer is reasonable: $150 − $147 = $3. Alana receives $3 in change. Since she paid only slightly more than the total cost, this answer makes sense.

9. Check your work. Since solving the problem took two steps, checking your work will take two steps. Add the amount of change Alana received to her total bill. This should equal how much she gave the cashier: $3 + $147 = $150. Divide Alana's total bill by 3. This should equal the cost of one pair of shoes: $147 ÷ 3 = $49.

It is also possible for a word problem to require the same operation to be performed more than once.

Example

Don owns three farms. Each farm has five chicken coops, and each chicken coop holds 25 chickens. If each chicken lays 6 eggs per week, how many eggs will Don have at the end of one week?

1. Read the entire word problem. You are given the number of eggs laid by a chicken in a week, the number of chickens in a chicken coop, the number of chicken coops on a farm, and the number of farms. You are looking for the total number of eggs laid.

2. Underline the keywords. The keyword *each* can signal multiplication or division, and this keyword appears in the word problem three times.

3. Cross out extra information and translate words into numbers. The numbers 3, 5, 25, and 6 will all be needed to solve the problem. In fact, even the number 1 (the number of weeks) is important. Multiplying by one won't change your answer, but if you were looking for the number of eggs laid in two weeks, then that number would be very important.

4. List the possible operations. You are given the number of farms and the number of chicken coops on each farm. You will need multiplication to find the total number of chicken coops. You are given the number of chickens in each coop, so you'll need multiplication again to find the total number of chickens. Once you have that number, you'll need multiplication one more time to find the number of eggs the chickens laid in a week. If you needed to find how many eggs the chickens laid in more than one week, you would need to multiply yet again!

5. Write number sentences for each operation. You'll form one multiplication sentence at a time, since you'll need your answer to each in order to form the next sentence. First, find the number of chicken coops on the three farms: 3×5.

6. Solve the number sentence and decide whether the answer is reasonable: $3 \times 5 = 15$.

    Now that you have the number of chicken coops, you can return to step 5 and find the total number of chickens.

7. Write number sentences for each operation. There are 15 chicken coops and 25 chickens in each coop, so the total number of chickens is equal to 15×25.

8. Solve the number sentence and decide whether the answer is reasonable: $15 \times 25 = 375$.

    Return to step 5 and use the total number of chickens to find the total number of eggs laid.

9. Write number sentences for each operation:

    There are 375 chickens, and each one lays 6 eggs per week, so the total number of eggs laid is equal to 375×6.

10. Solve the number sentence and decide whether the answer is reasonable: $375 \times 6 = 2,250$.

    Since you are looking for the number of eggs laid in one week, you have your answer.

11. Check your work. You multiplied three times to find your answer, so you will check your work by dividing three times. Divide the total number of eggs by the number of eggs laid by each chicken. This should equal the number of chickens: 2,250 ÷ 6 = 375. Divide the number of chickens by the number of chickens in each coop. This should equal the number of chicken coops: 375 ÷ 25 = 15. Finally divide the number of chicken coops by the number of chicken coops on each farm. This should equal the number of farms: 15 ÷ 3 = 5.

Practice

Solve the following word problems. Show your work using the steps.

25. Rikin has $328 in his bank account. He deposits $103, and then takes $66 out of the account. How much money is in Rikin's account now?

26. A truck delivers newspapers to 24 newsstands. Each newsstand receives 50 newspapers. If each newspaper costs $0.50, and all the newspapers are sold, how much money will the newsstands collect?

27. One package of paper contains 140 sheets. Jason's report is 6 pages long, and he must make one copy for each student in the ninth grade. If there are 210 students in the ninth grade, how many packages of paper does Jason need?

28. A pizzeria charges $1.85 for a slice of pizza and $1.25 for a drink. Ted buys two slices of pizza and a drink, and pays with a five-dollar bill. How much change does he receive?

29. A cooler holds 280 ounces of water. Michelle uses the cooler to fill 18 eight-ounce cups of water, and then fills a 36-ounce pitcher. How much water is left in the cooler?

Whenever you must use more than one operation to solve a problem, you need to be careful about the order in which you do those operations. Sometimes the order of the operations is easy to spot based on the context of the problem, but when a word problem is strictly about numbers, it can be more difficult. For problems like this, you must read carefully and break the problem into pieces.

Example
What is three less than twice four?

You can use the seven-step process to solve problems like this, but first, let's focus on each word of the problem. You are asked to find three less than twice four. Before you can find three less than twice four, you must first find twice four. Twice four is the same as two times four. Once you have found two times four, you can find three less than that by subtracting three. This problem, written numerically, is $(2 \times 4) - 3$. Now that you know what the problem is asking us, you don't need the seven-step process—it's not a word problem anymore: $(2 \times 4) - 3 = 8 - 3 = 5$. Three less than twice four is five.

Practice

Solve the following word problems. Show your work using the steps.

30. Find the quotient of 96 and three less than eleven.

31. What is five more than the product of six and eight?

32. What number is sixteen times the sum of two and ten?

33. Find the difference between twenty and twice seven.

34. What is nineteen multiplied by twelve divided by four?

35. Find the sum of six dozen and six less than twelve.

36. What is the product of seven fewer than thirteen and five squared?

37. What is the product of four and six less than ten, divided by two?

38. Find the difference between eight more than seventeen and eight less than seventeen.

39. What is the product of the difference between sixteen and nine and the sum of eleven and twice five?

Answers

1. The keyword *product* signals multiplication. $15 \times 9 = 135$.

2. The problem contains the keyword phrase *more than* (even though the word *cases* is in between the words *more* and *than*). Since Dean has 19 more cases than Andrea, you must add 19 to the number of cases Andrea has (33) to find the number of cases Dean has: $33 + 19 = 52$ cases.

3. The keywords in this problem are *share* and *each*. *Each* can signal multiplication or division, but the keyword *share* always signals division. Since 20 students are sharing 220 books, each student will receive less than 220 books. You must divide 220 by 20 to find how many books each student will receive: $220 \div 20 = 11$ books.

4. The keyword *every* signals multiplication. If one bull's eye hit is 45 points, then two bull's eye hits will be more than 45 points—two times more. Multiply the value of a bull's eye hit by the number of times Matt hits the bull's eye: $45 \times 14 = 630$ points.

5. The keyword *increased* signals addition. To increase 25 by 37, you must add 37 to 25: $25 + 37 = 62$.

6. The keyword *per* can signal multiplication or division. In this problem, you are given a number of skiers and how much they all paid for lift tickets. The cost of a ticket per person will be less than $420, so you are looking for an operation that can be performed on $420 that will make that value smaller. You must divide $420 by 12 to find the cost of a ticket per person: $420 \div 12 = 35. Each skier paid $35.

7. The keyword *remain* signals subtraction. The store had 55 snow shovels, but has fewer now that it has sold some of them. To find how many snow shovels remain, you must subtract the number of shovels sold from the original number of shovels: 55 − 38 = 17 shovels.

8. The keyword *quotient* signals division. Divide 126 by 42: 126 ÷ 42 = 3.

9. The keyword *altogether* signals addition. Add the number of goals scored by Maurice to the number of goals scored by Steve to find how many goals they scored combined: 37 + 24 = 61 goals.

10. The keyword *left* signals subtraction. Natila's original total of 75 euros decreases after she spends 59 euros. Subtract 59 from 75: 75 − 59 = 16 euros.

11. *Read the entire word problem.*

You are given the total distance of a race, the number of athletes, and you're looking for how far each athlete runs.
Underline the keywords.

The word *each* is a keyword.
List the possible operations.

The keyword can signal either multiplication or division.
Write number sentences for each operation.

Since multiplication is commutative (the order of the factors does not matter), you only have one multiplication number sentence: 5 × 1,000. You have two division number sentences: 5 ÷ 1,000 and 1,000 ÷ 5.
Solve the number sentences and decide which answer is reasonable.

5 × 1,000 = 5,000, 5 ÷ 1,000 = 0.005, 1,000 ÷ 5 = 200. The total distance of the race is 1,000 meters, so it would be impossible for each athlete to run 5,000 meters. Each athlete must run less than 1,000 meters. The number 0.005 is very small. Since there are only 5 athletes, if each ran 0.005 meters, they would be unable to finish the race! It sounds reasonable that each athlete would run 200

meters, since this number is less than 1,000, but not too small.
Check your work.

Since you used division to find the answer to this problem, you must use multiplication to check your work. If each athlete runs 200 meters and there are 5 athletes, then 200 × 5 = 1,000, which is the total distance of the race. 200 meters is the correct answer.

12. *Read the entire word problem.*

You are given the number of products produced in one hour and you are looking for the number of products produced in 7 hours.
Underline the keywords.

Even though *product* is sometimes a keyword, it is not being used as a direction for an operation here. So, there are no keywords in this word problem, and you will need to use the context of the problem to determine which operation to use.
List the possible operations.

If the machine produces 420 products in one hour, it will produce more than 420 products in more than one hour. You are looking for an operation that will make the number 420 larger. Multiplication and addition will both make the number 420 larger.
Write number sentences for each operation.

Since addition and multiplication are both commutative, you only have one number sentence for each operation: 420 × 7 and 420 + 7.
Solve the number sentences and decide which answer is reasonable.

420 × 7 = 2,940, 420 + 7 = 427. 427 is too small. If the machine produces 420 products in the first hour, it would produce 420 products in the second hour, for a total of 840 in two hours. In 7 hours, it would produce much more than 427 products. Since the machine produces 420 products each hour, multiplication is the right operation to use. 2,940 is a reasonable answer.

Check your work.

Since you used multiplication to find the answer to this problem, you must use division to check your work. If the machine produces a total of 2,940 products in 7 hours, then the number of products it produces in one hour should be equal to 2,940 divided by 7: $2,940 \div 7 = 420$.

13. *Read the entire word problem.*

You are given the size of Jonathan's disc and the number of megabytes used on the disc. you are looking for the number of megabytes that are remaining.

Underline the keywords.

The word *remaining* is a keyword.

List the possible operations.

The keyword *remaining* signals subtraction.

Write number sentences for each operation.

We have two subtraction number sentences you can write using these numbers: $1,440 - 865$ and $865 - 1,440$.

Solve the number sentences and decide which answer is reasonable.

$1,440 - 865 = 575$ and $865 - 1,440 = -575$. The number of megabytes remaining on the disc won't be a negative number, since that would be impossible. Since the disc holds 1,440 megabytes and 865 megabytes are used, the number of remaining megabytes is the positive difference between those two numbers. 575 megabytes is a reasonable answer.

Check your work.

Since you used subtraction to find the answer to this problem, you must use addition to check your work. If 865 megabytes are used and 575 megabytes remain, the total size of the disc, 1,440, should be equal to the sum of 865 and 575: $865 + 575 = 1,440$, so our answer is correct.

14. Read the entire word problem.

You are given the number of deliveries made in two different weeks. You are looking for the total number of deliveries made in those two weeks.

Underline the keywords.

The word *altogether* is a keyword.

List the possible operations.

The keyword *altogether* signals addition.

Write number sentences for each operation.

Since addition is commutative, you only have one number sentence to write: $18 + 24$.

Solve the number sentence and decide whether the answer is reasonable.

$18 + 24 = 42$ deliveries.

Check your work.

Since you used addition to find the answer to this problem, you must use subtraction to check your work. If 42 deliveries were made altogether, then the total minus the number of deliveries made last week, 18, should equal the number of deliveries made this week, 24: $42 - 18 = 24$.

15. Read the entire word problem.

You are given the number of laps Allie swam in one day and the number of days she swam. You are looking for the number of laps she swam in 15 days.

Underline the keywords.

The word *every* is a keyword.

List the possible operations.

The keyword *every* signals multiplication, although "every," like "each," can sometimes signal division.

Write number sentences for each operation.

We have one multiplication sentence and two division sentences to write: 55×15, $55 \div 15$, and $15 \div 55$.

Solve the number sentences and decide which answer is reasonable.

$55 \times 15 = 825$, $55 \div 15$ is approximately 3.7, and $15 \div 55$ is approximately 0.27. The decimal answers do not make sense, since Allie swims a whole number of laps every day, which means that the number of laps she would swim over 15 days would also be a whole number. Multiplication makes sense, since you are given the number of laps she swims in one day and you are looking for the number of laps she swims for more than one day. 825 is a reasonable answer.

Check your work.

Since you used multiplication to find the answer to this problem, you must use division to check your work. If Allie swims 825 laps in 15 days, then 825 divided by 15 should give you the number of laps Allie swims in one day: $825 \div 15 = 55$.

16. *Read the entire word problem.*

You are given the total number of cards in a box and the number of cards used by Emma. You are looking for the number of cards left in the box.

Underline the keywords.

The word *left* is a keyword.

List the possible operations.

The keyword *left* signals subtraction.

Write number sentences for each operation.

We have two subtraction number sentences you can write using these numbers: $625 - 313$ and $313 - 625$.

Solve the number sentences and decide which answer is reasonable.

$625 - 313 = 312$ and $313 - 625 = -312$. The number of cards left in the box can't be a negative number, since that would be impossible. Since the box began with 625 cards and 313 cards are used, the number of cards left is the positive difference between those two numbers. 312 cards is a reasonable answer.

Check your work.

Since you used subtraction to find the answer to this problem, you must use addition to check your work. If 313 cards are used and 312 cards are left, the total size of the box, 625, should be equal to the sum of 313 and 312: $313 + 312 = 625$.

17. *Read the entire word problem.*

You are given the number of rolls of nickels Ethan has and the number of nickels in each roll. You are looking for the number of nickels in 12 rolls.

Underline the keywords.

The word *each* is a keyword.

List the possible operations.

The keyword *each* could signal multiplication or division.

Write number sentences for each operation.

You have one multiplication sentence and two division sentences to write: 12×40, $12 \div 40$, and $40 \div 12$.

Solve the number sentences and decide which answer is reasonable.

$12 \times 40 = 480$, $12 \div 40 = 0.3$ and $40 \div 12$ is approximately 3.3. The decimal answers do not make sense, since the number of nickels in a roll is a whole number and the number of rolls is a whole number. Multiplication makes sense, since you are given the number of nickels in one roll and you are looking for the number of nickels in 12 rolls. 480 is a reasonable answer.

Check your work.

Since you used multiplication to find the answer to this problem, you must use division to check your work. If there are 480 nickels in 12 rolls, then the number of nickels in one roll is equal to 480 divided by 12: $480 \div 12 = 40$.

18. *Read the entire word problem.*

You are given the total number of minutes of footage and the number of days over which the footage was recorded. You are looking for the number of minutes each day.

Underline the keywords.

The word *each* is a keyword.

List the possible operations.

The keyword tells you you'll need to use either multiplication or division.

Write number sentences for each operation.

You have one multiplication number sentence: $1,565 \times 5$. You have two division number sentences: $1,565 \div 5$ and $5 \div 1,565$.

Solve the number sentences and decide which answer is reasonable.

$1,565 \times 5 = 7,825$, $1,565 \div 5 = 313$, $5 \div 1,565$ is approximately 0.003. David records a total of 1,565 minutes of footage in 5 days, which means that the number of minutes recorded each day is less than 1,565, so multiplication is not the right operation. The number 0.003 is too small to be the number of minutes David recorded each day, because at that rate, he'd have to record for 1,000 days just to record 3 minutes of footage. 313 minutes is a reasonable number of minutes for each of the 5 days, since it is less than 1,565 but not too small.

Check your work.

Since you used division to find the answer to this problem, you must use multiplication to check your work. If David records 313 minutes each day for 5 days, then the total number of minutes of footage is equal to the product of 313 and 5: $313 \times 5 = 1,565$.

19. *Read the entire word problem.*

You are given the starting weight of the polar bear and the number of pounds the bear loses. You are looking for the weight of the bear now.

Underline the keywords.

None of the keywords you learned in Chapter 3 appear in this problem, so you will have to use the context of the word problem.

List the possible operations.

The polar bear loses 45 pounds over the course of the year, which means that the bear's weight decreases. You need to use an operation that lowers the number 903, such as subtraction or division.

Write number sentences for each operation.

You have two subtraction number sentences and two division sentences: $903 - 45$, $45 - 903$, $903 \div 45$, and $45 \div 903$.

Solve the number sentences and decide which answer is reasonable.

$903 - 45 = 858$, $45 - 903 = -858$, $903 \div 45$ is approximately 20.067, and $45 \div 903$ is approximately 0.05. The weight of the bear can't be negative, so the answer -858 is wrong. The bear would have had to lose almost all its weight to weigh either 20.067 or 0.05 pounds. The only reasonable answer is 858 pounds. This weight is 45 pounds less than the starting weight of the bear.

Check your work.

Since you used subtraction to find the answer to this problem, you must use addition to check your work. If the bear weighs 858 pounds after losing 45 pounds, then the original weight of the bear is equal to the sum of its original weight and the number of pounds it lost: $858 + 45 = 903$ pounds.

20. *Read the entire word problem.*

You are given the amount of time Monica rides the subway, the amount of time she walks, and the speed of the subway. You are looking for the total time it takes Monica to get to work.

Underline the keywords.

There are no keywords in this problem, so you will have to use the context of the word problem.

Cross out extra information.

Since you are looking for the total time it takes Monica to get to work, you don't need the average speed of the subway. Cross out that part of the word problem.

List the possible operations.

To find the time it takes Monica to get to work, you need to combine the time she spends on the subway and the time she spends walking. You need to use addition.

Write number sentences for each operation.

You have just one addition number sentence: 35 + 13.

Solve the number sentence and decide whether the answer is reasonable.

35 + 13 = 48. Since this number is not too large, but still greater than both the time Monica spends on the subway and the time she spends walking, this answer is reasonable.

Check your work.

Since you used addition to find the answer to this problem, you must use subtraction to check your work. If it takes Monica 48 minutes to get to work, then the number of minutes she spends walking should be equal to the total time minus the number of minutes she spends on the subway: 48 − 35 = 13 minutes.

21. *Read the entire word problem.*

You are given the cost of a stamp, the number of stamps Lisa buys, and the number of packages she mails. You are looking for the amount of money Lisa spends on stamps.

Underline the keywords.

There are no keywords in this problem, so you will have to use the context of the word problem.

Cross out extra information.

Since you are looking for the amount of money Lisa spends on stamps, you don't need to know how many packages she sent. Cross out that part of the word problem.

List the possible operations.

The cost of 25 stamps is greater than the cost of one stamp. You need to choose an operation that makes the number 44 larger, such as addition or multiplication.

Write number sentences for each operation.

You have one addition number sentence and one multiplication sentence: 44 + 25 and 44 × 25.

Solve the number sentences and decide which answer is reasonable.

44 + 25 = 69 and 44 × 25 = 1,100. 69 cents is too small; the cost of two stamps would be more than 69 cents, since 44 + 44 = 88. Multiplying the number of stamps by the price of one stamp is the correct operation. Lisa spends 1,100 cents, or $11.00, on stamps.

Check your work.

Since you used multiplication to find the answer to this problem, you must use division to check your work. If the cost of 25 stamps is 1,100 cents, then the cost of one stamp is equal to 1,100 divided by 25: 1,100 ÷ 25 = 44.

22. *Read the entire word problem.*

You are given the distance each girl flies and the time each girl spends flying. You are looking for the difference between the distances the girls fly.

Underline the keywords.

The phrase *farther than* (although it is split up by other words) signals subtraction.

Cross out extra information.

Since you are looking for the difference between the distances the girls fly, you don't need to know how long they spent flying. Cross out the numbers of hours.

List the possible operations.

To find how much farther Lindsay flies than Jamie flies, you must use subtraction.

Write number sentences for each operation.

You have two subtraction sentences: $2{,}462 - 719$ and $719 - 2{,}462$.

Solve the number sentences and decide which answer is reasonable.

$2{,}462 - 719 = 1{,}743$ and $719 - 2{,}462 = -1{,}743$. The difference between their distances cannot be negative, so 1,743 must be the correct answer. It is less than the larger of the two distances, so it is a reasonable answer.

Check your work.

Since you used subtraction to find the answer to this problem, you must use addition to check your work. If Lindsay flew 1,743 miles more than Jamie, then the sum of that distance and the distance Jamie flew must be equal to the distance Lindsay flew: $1{,}743 + 719 = 2{,}462$ miles.

23. *Read the entire word problem.*

You are given the number of seats in the hall, the number of seats sold, and the cost of one ticket. You are looking for the total amount of money collected.

Underline the keywords.

The word *per* is a keyword.

Cross out extra information.

Since you are looking for the amount of money collected, you only need the number of seats sold and the cost of a ticket. you don't need to know how many seats there are in the concert hall, so cross out that number.

List the possible operations.

The keyword *per* can signal multiplication or division.

Write number sentences for each operation.

You have one multiplication sentence and two division sentences: $3{,}216 \times 18$, $3{,}216 \div 18$, and $18 \div 3{,}216$.

Solve the number sentences and decide which answer is reasonable.

$3{,}216 \times 18 = 57{,}888$, $3{,}216 \div 18$ is about 178.67 and $18 \div 3{,}216$ is about 0.006. The results of the division number sentences are not reasonable. The total amount of money collected will be more than the cost of one ticket since more than one ticket was sold. Since you are given the cost of one ticket and need to find the cost of many tickets, you must use multiplication. $57,888 is a reasonable answer.

Check your work.

Since you used multiplication to find the answer to this problem, you must use division to check your work. If the total collected by the concert hall is $57,888, then that total divided by the ticket price, $18, must equal the number of seats sold: $\$57{,}888 \div \$18 = 3{,}216$.

24. *Read the entire word problem.*

You are given the number of students that attended last year, the increase in enrollment, and the cost of tuition. You are looking for the number of students attending this year.

Underline the keywords.

The word *increase* is a keyword.

Cross out extra information.

Since you are looking for the number of students attending this year, you don't need to know the increase in the cost of tuition. Cross out that number.

List the possible operations.

The keyword *increase* signals addition. You need to add the number of students that attended last year to size of the increase.

Write number sentences for each operation.

We have just one addition sentence: 2,314 + 239.

Solve the number sentence and decide whether the answer is reasonable.

2,314 + 239 = 2,553. The new number of students attending is larger than the old number of students that attended the college, so this answer is reasonable.

Check your work.

Since you used addition to find the answer to this problem, you must use subtraction to check your work. If the new number of students attending Lincoln College is 2,553, then that number minus the increase should be equal to the number of students that attended the college last year: 2,553 − 239 = 2,314.

25. *Read the entire word problem.*

You are given how much Rikin has in his account, how much he deposits, and how much he takes out. You are looking for how much money he has in his account now.

Underline the keywords.

There are no keywords in this problem, but a deposit increases the amount of money in an account, and taking money out decreases that total.

Cross out extra information and translate words into numbers.

There is no extra information and there are no words to translate into numbers.

List the possible operations.

Since a deposit increases the amount in Rikin's account, you must add $103 to his account. When he takes $66 out of the account, you must subtract $66 from his total.

Write number sentences for each operation.

Write the addition number sentence first; you will use this sum in our subtraction sentence. $328 + $103.

Solve the number sentence and decide whether the answer is reasonable.

$328 + $103 = $431. You expected your answer to be greater than $328, so this answer is reasonable.

Write number sentences for each operation.

Now write the subtraction number sentence using the sum you just found: $431 − $66.

Solve the number sentence and decide whether the answer is reasonable.

$431 − $66 = $365.

Check your work.

You added and then subtracted to find your answer, so you will check your work by adding (the opposite of subtracting) and then subtracting (the opposite of adding). Adding the amount Rikin took out of his account to his final total should give you the amount in his account after his deposit: $365 + $66 =

$431. Subtracting the deposit from this total should give you the original amount of money in Rikin's account: $431 − $103 = $328.

26. *Read the entire word problem.*

You are given the number of newsstands, the number of newspapers at each newsstand, and the price of each newspaper. You are looking for the total money collected.

Underline the keywords.

The keyword *each* can signal multiplication or division, and it appears twice in the problem.

Cross out extra information and translate words into numbers.

There is no extra information and there are no words to translate into numbers.

List the possible operations.

Since one newsstand receives 50 newspapers, you will need to multiply the number of newsstands by 50 to find the total number of newspapers delivered. Once you have that number, you can multiply it by the price of one newspaper.

Write number sentences for each operation.

24 × 50.

Solve the number sentence and decide whether the answer is reasonable.

24 × 50 = 1,200.

Write number sentences for each operation.

There are 1,200 newspapers and each costs $0.50. The total money collected is equal to the product of 1,200 and $0.50.

Solve the number sentence and decide whether the answer is reasonable.

1,200 × $0.50 = $600.

Check your work.

You multiplied twice to find your answer, so you will check your work by dividing twice. Divide the total money collected by the price of one newspaper, and this should give you the number of newspapers sold: $600 ÷ $0.50 = 1,200. Divide the number of newspapers sold by the number of newspapers delivered to each

newsstand. This should give you the number of newsstands: 1,200 ÷ 50 = 24 newsstands.

27. *Read the entire word problem.*

You are given the number of sheets of paper in a package, the length of Jason's report, and the number of students in the ninth grade. You are looking for the number of packages of paper Jason needs.

Underline the keywords.

The keyword *each* can signal multiplication or division.

Cross out extra information and translate words into numbers.

There is no extra information and there are no words to translate into numbers.

List the possible operations.

If one copy of Jason's report is 6 pages, and he needs to make 210 copies of his report, you need to multiply to find the total number of pages Jason needs.

Write number sentences for each operation.

6 × 210.

Solve the number sentence and decide whether the answer is reasonable.

6 × 210 = 1,260.

Write number sentences for each operation.

One package of paper contains 140 sheets, so the number of packages of paper that Jason needs is equal to 1,260 ÷ 140.

Solve the number sentence and decide whether the answer is reasonable.

1,260 ÷ 140 = 9 packages.

Check your work.

You multiplied and divided to find your answer, so you will divide and multiply to check your work. Multiply the number of packages, 9, by the number of sheets in a package, 140. This should equal the total number of sheets Jason needs: 9 × 140 = 1,260. Divide this product by the number of students in the ninth grade, 210, and this should equal the length of Jason's report: 1,260 ÷ 210 = 6 pages.

28. *Read the entire word problem.*

You are given the price of a slice of pizza, the price of a drink, the number of slices and the number of drinks Ted buys, and how much he pays. You are looking for the change he receives.

Underline the keywords.

There are no keywords in this problem, but the word *change* often signals subtraction.

Cross out extra information and translate words into numbers.

There is no extra information and there are no words to translate into numbers.

List the possible operations.

First, you must find how much Ted spent. Begin by multiplying the number of slices Ted bought by the price of each slice.

Write number sentences for each operation.

2 × $1.85.

Solve the number sentence and decide whether the answer is reasonable.

2 × $1.85 = $3.70.

Write number sentences for each operation.

Next, find the total amount Ted spent by adding the cost of the drink: $3.70 + $1.25.

Solve the number sentence and decide whether the answer is reasonable.

$3.70 + $1.25 = $4.95. Now that you have the total amount that Ted spent, you can find how much change he received by subtracting that total from the amount Ted paid, $5.

Write number sentences for each operation.

$5.00 − $4.95.

Solve the number sentence and decide whether the answer is reasonable.

$5.00 − $4.95 = $0.05.

Check your work.

You multiplied, added, and subtracted to find your answer, so you will add, subtract, and divide to check your work. Add the change Ted received to his total amount spent, and this should equal the amount Ted paid: $0.05 +

$4.95 = $5.00. Subtract from Ted's bill the cost of the drink, and this should equal how much Ted paid for the two slices of pizza: $4.95 − $1.25 = $3.70. Finally divide that total by two, and the answer should equal the price of one slice of pizza: $3.70 ÷ 2 = $1.85.

29. *Read the entire word problem.*

You are given the number of ounces in the cooler, the number of cups of water filled, the size of each cup, and the number of ounces used to fill a pitcher. You are looking for the amount of water left in the cooler.

Underline the keywords.

The keyword *left* signals subtraction.

Cross out extra information and translate words into numbers.

There is no extra information and there are no words to translate into numbers.

List the possible operations.

In order to find how much water is left in the cooler, you must first figure out how much water was poured into the cups. Since there are 18 cups, and one cup holds 8 ounces, you must multiply 18 by 8 to find how many ounces were used to fill the cups.

Write number sentences for each operation.

18 × 8.

Solve the number sentence and decide whether the answer is reasonable.

18 × 8 = 144.

Write number sentences for each operation.

Subtract 144 ounces from the total volume in the cooler, 280 ounces.

Solve the number sentence and decide whether the answer is reasonable.

280 − 144 = 136 ounces. You don't have the answer yet. You still need to subtract the 36 ounces Michelle poured into the pitcher.

Write number sentences for each operation.

136 − 36.

Solve the number sentence and decide whether the answer is reasonable.

136 − 36 = 100 ounces.

Check your work.

You multiplied and then subtracted twice to find our answer. You will add twice and divide to check your work. Add the number of ounces poured into the pitcher to the final volume of the cooler: 100 + 36 = 136. Add the number of ounces in the 18 cups to this sum, and that should give you the original amount of water in the cooler: 136 + 144 = 280 ounces. You can check that your multiplication was correct by dividing the total volume of the cups, 144 ounces, by the number of ounces in each cup, 8, and that should give you the number of cups: 18: 144 ÷ 8 = 18 cups.

30. You are looking for the quotient of 96 and a number: 96 ÷ ( ). That number is three less than eleven, which is 11 − 3. 96 ÷ (11 − 3) = 96 ÷ 8 = 12.

31. You are looking for 5 more than a number: 5 + ( ). That number is the product of six and eight, which is 6 × 8. 5 + (6 × 8) = 5 + 48 = 53.

32. You are looking for 16 times a number: 16 × ( ). That number is the sum of two and ten, which is 2 + 10. 16 × (2 + 10) = 16 × 12 = 192.

33. You are looking for the difference between 20 and a number: 20 − ( ). That number is twice seven, which is 2 × 7. 20 − (2 × 7) = 20 − 14 = 6.

34. You can either multiply 19 by 12 and then divide by 4, or, you can divide 12 by 4 and then multiply by 19. In this problem, the order does not matter. Let's start by dividing, since it will make the numbers easier to work with. 19 × (12 ÷ 4) = 19 × 3 = 57.

35. You are looking for the sum of two numbers: ( ) + ( ). The first number is six dozen, which is 6 × 12. The second number is six less than twelve, which is 12 − 6. The problem is now (6 × 12) + (12 − 6) = 72 + 6 = 78.

36. You are looking for the product of two numbers: ( ) × ( ). The first number is seven fewer than thirteen, which is 13 − 7. The second number is five squared, which is 5^2. The problem is now $(13 - 7) \times (5^2) = 6 \times 25 = 150$.

37. You are looking for the product of two numbers divided by two: [( ) × ( )] ÷ 2. The first number is four. The second number is six less than ten, or 10 − 6. The problem is now [(4) × (10 − 6)] ÷ 2 = (4 × 4) ÷ 2 = 16 ÷ 2 = 8.

38. You are looking for the difference between two numbers: ( ) − ( ). The first number is eight more than seventeen, which is 17 + 8. The second number is eight less than seventeen, which is 17 − 8. The problem is now (17 + 8) − (17 − 8) = 25 − 9 = 16.

39. You are looking for the product of two numbers: ( ) × ( ). The first number is the difference between sixteen and nine, which is 16 − 9. The second number is the sum of two numbers. The first is 11 and the second is twice five, or 2 × 5. The problem is now (16 − 9) × [11 + (2 × 5)] = 7 × (11 + 10) = 7 × 21 = 147.

9 ▶ Graphs

In this chapter, you will be visually introduced to the many graphs used to display data, including tables, bar graphs, line graphs, scatter plots, circle graphs, and pictographs.

Graphs are incredibly useful because they communicate information visually. You probably have read graphs in newspapers, magazines, or online. When complicated information is difficult to understand, an illustration—or graph—can help get your point across quickly. That's one reason you're likely to find graphs on your law enforcement exam, and a good reason to understand how to read them.

Circle Graphs

Circle graphs show how the parts of a whole relate to one another. A circle graph is a circle divided into slices or wedges. Each slice represents a category. Circle graphs are sometimes called pie charts.

Example

Recycled Material Collected for One Month

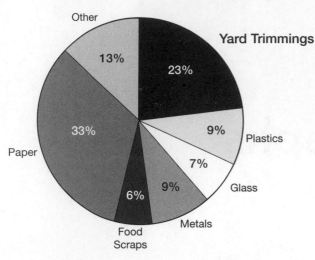

This circle graph classifies materials that were collected for recycling into distinct categories. Based on the circle graph, which category represents the largest part of the collection?

Look at all the slices of the circle graph. You can see that paper represents the largest slice, or 33%.

Practice

The following circle graph represents data collected from a recent telephone survey.

How Federal Dollars Are Spent

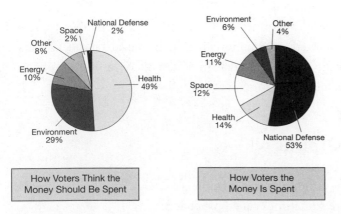

Using the "How Federal Dollars Are Spent" circle graph, answer the following questions.

1. Based on the survey, which category of spending best matches the voters' wishes?

2. On which category of spending did the voters want most of the money spent?

3. Which category of spending receives the most federal dollars?

4. To which two categories of spending did voters want the most money to go? Which two categories of spending actually received the most money?

Bar Graphs

Like circle graphs, **bar graphs** show how different categories of data relate to one another. Bar graphs can be used to present one type of data or may contain different colored bars that allow for a side-by-side comparison of similar statistics.

A bar represents each category. The height of the bar represents the relative frequency of the category, compared to the other categories on the graph.

When reading a bar graph there are several things you must pay attention to: the title, two axes, the bars, and the scale (if there is one). The title gives an overview of the information being presented in the bar graph. The title is usually given at the top of the graph.

Each bar graph has two axes, which are labeled. The axes labels inform you what information is presented on each axis. One axis represents data groups; the other represents the frequency of the data groups.

The bars are rectangular blocks that can have their base at either vertical axis or horizontal axis. Each bar represents the data for one of the data groups.

Example

Employee Anniversaries by Month

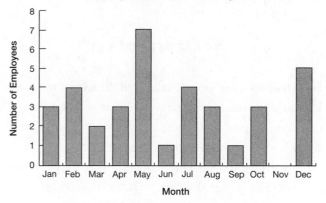

This bar graph shows the number of employees at a company who have an anniversary during any given month. Based on the bar graph, how many months have three anniversaries celebrated?

Look at 3 on the vertical axis, which represents the number of employees. You can see that the following months on the horizontal axis reach the 3: January, April, August, and October. So, during four months, three anniversaries are celebrated.

Practice

The following bar graph compares the 2009 rainfall amounts in Cherokee County with the average rainfall in Cherokee County over the last five years.

Rainfall in Cherokee County

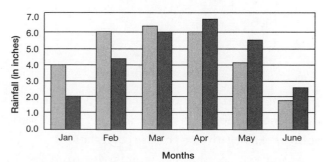

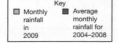

Using the "Rainfall in Cherokee County" bar graph, answer the following questions.

5. What does each bar represent? What is the difference between the shaded bars and the white bars?

6. During which month(s) was the rainfall in 2009 greater than the average rainfall over the five previous years?

7. During which month(s) was the rainfall in 2009 less than the average rainfall over the five previous years?

8. How many more inches of rain fell in April 2009 than in January 2009?

9. How many more inches of rain fell in January 2009 than on average during the last five years in January?

Line Graphs

Line graphs show how two categories of data or information (sometimes called **variables**) relate to one another. The data is displayed on a grid and is presented on a scale using a horizontal and a vertical axis for the different categories of information compared on the graph. Usually, each data point is connected together to form a line so that you can see trends in the data and so that you can see how the data changes over time. Often you will see line graphs with *time* on the horizontal axis. It may help to think of a line graph as being formed by connecting the topmost points of vertical bars on a bar graph and then erasing the bars.

Line graphs are good to display information that continues, such as temperatures or snowfall.

Example

Average Temperatures

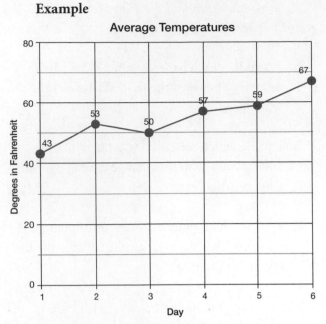

Practice

Consider the following information.

How People Get to Work

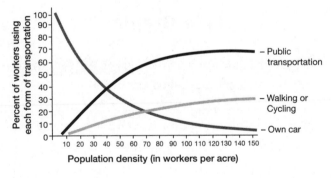

Using the "How People Get to Work" line graph, answer the following questions.

10. What variable is shown on the vertical axis? What variable is shown on the horizontal axis?

11. As the population density increases, will more or fewer people drive their own car to work?

12. At about what point in population density does the use of public transportation begin to level off?

13. Which form of transportation becomes less popular as population density increases?

Scatterplots

Scatterplots have points scattered all over the place. Like line graphs, scatterplots use horizontal and vertical axes to plot data points. However, scatterplots show how much one variable is affected by another.

Scatterplots usually consist of a large body of data. The closer the data points come when plotted to making a straight line, the higher the connection between the two variables, or the stronger the relationship.

If the data points make a straight line rising from left to right, then the variables have a positive correlation.

If the line goes from a high value on the left down to a right axis, the variables have a negative correlation.

Example

Relationship between Income and Years of Experience

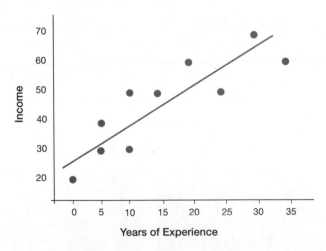

The scatterplot shows how a person's years of experience relate to his or her income. Do the variables have a negative or positive correlation?

You can see the data points rise from left to right, so the variables have a positive correlation.

Pictographs

Instead of using lines, bars, or chunks of pie to represent data, **pictographs** use pictures. You may see these types of graphs in newspapers and magazines. Each picture on a pictograph represents a quantity of something. There is a key to tell you what each picture means.

Example

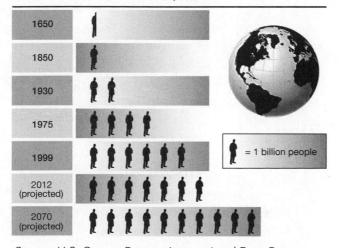

World Population

= 1 billion people

Source: U.S. Census Bureau. International Data Base.

Getting Information from Tables

Tables are used to organize information into columns and rows. Usually, a description of the data presented is located at the top of the table. Rows go across, or horizontally. Columns go up and down, or vertically. The box, or cell, that is made where a row and a column meet provides specific information.

Before looking to the particulars of the data, you should ask yourself, "What is this table telling me?" By focusing on what the table means to tell you, you will be able to find the data that you need more easily, and analyze it accordingly.

Example

WORKPLACE PERFORMANCE ISSUES		
SPECIFIC PERFORMANCE ISSUE	EMPLOYEE COMMITTING INFRACTION	DEALING WITH PERFORMANCE ISSUE
Lateness, absenteeism, leaving without permission	Mario	Oral warning
Poor prioritizing, timing, scheduling	Kyle	Written warning
Destructive humor, sarcasm, horseplay, fighting	Pat	Suspension
Threatening, hostile, or intimidating behaviors	Kevin	Termination

Practice

Using the Fujita-Pearson Tornado Intensity Scale, answer the questions that follow.

THE FUJITA-PEARSON TORNADO INTENSITY SCALE		
CLASSIFICATION	WIND SPEED (IN MILES PER HOUR)	DAMAGE
F0	72	Mild
F1	73–112	Moderate
F2	113–157	Significant
F3	158–206	Severe
F4	207–260	Devastating
F5	261–319	Cataclysmic
F6	320–379	Overwhelming

14. If a tornado has a wind speed of 173 miles per hour, how would it be classified?

15. What kind of damage would you expect from a tornado having a wind speed of 300 miles per hour?

16. What wind speed would you anticipate if a tornado of F6 were reported?

Answers

1. Energy: Voters say they'd like about 10% of the budget spent on energy and about 11% is spent on energy.
2. Health
3. National defense
4. Voters wanted money to go to health and environment. National defense and health received the most money.
5. Look at the labels and the key. Each bar represents the number of inches of rainfall during a particular month. From the key, you know that the shaded bars represent the average monthly rainfall for 2004 through 2008. The white bars represent the rainfall in 2009.

6. Compare the white bars with the shaded bars. Rainfall in 2009 is greater than average during the months that the white bar is taller than the shaded bar for that month. Rainfall in 2009 was greater than the average rainfall during January, February, and March.

7. Compare the white bars with the shaded bars. Rainfall in 2009 is less than average during the months that the shaded bar is taller than the white bar for that month. Rainfall in 2009 was less than the average rainfall during April, May, and June.

8. Compare the height of the white bars for January and April. In April, 6 inches of rain fell. In January, 4 inches of rain fell. Then subtract: 6 – 4 = 2. So, in April, 2 more inches of rain fell than in January.

9. Compare the height of the shaded bar and the white bar for January. The shaded bar represents 2 inches. The white bar represents 4 inches. Subtract: 4 – 2 = 2. So, two more inches of rain fell in January 2009 than on average during the last five years in January.

10. Look at the labels. The percent of workers using each form of transportation is shown on the vertical axis. Population density is shown on the horizontal axis.

11. As population density increases, fewer people use their own cars to get to work.

12. At about 80 to 100 workers per acre, the percentage of workers using public transportation begins to level off at about 70%.

13. Find the line that moves down as population density increases. It's the line labeled "own car." This is the form of transportation that decreases as population density increases.

14. F3. The wind speed for F3 tornados ranges from 158 to 206 mph.

15. Cataclysmic: F5 tornados range in wind speed from 261 to 319 mph and are *cataclysmic*.

16. F6 tornados range in wind speeds from 320 to 379 miles per hour.

10 ▶ Measurement

This chapter reviews the basics of measurement systems used in the United States and other countries, methods of performing mathematical operations with units of measurement, and the process of converting between different units.

The use of measurement enables a connection to be made between mathematics and the real world. To measure any object, assign a number and a unit of measure. For example, when a fish is caught, it is often weighed in ounces and its length measured in inches. The following review will help you become more familiar with the types, conversions, and units of measurement.

Types of Measurements

Here are the types of measurements used most frequently in the United States.

Units of Length

12 inches (in.) = 1 foot (ft.)

3 feet = 36 inches = 1 yard (yd.)

5,280 feet = 1,760 yards = 1 mile (mi.)

Units of Volume

8 ounces* (oz.) = 1 cup (c.)

2 cups = 16 ounces = 1 pint (pt.)

2 pints = 4 cups = 32 ounces = 1 quart (qt.)

4 quarts = 8 pints = 16 cups = 128 ounces = 1 gallon (gal.)

Units of Weight

16 ounces* (oz.) = 1 pound (lb.)

2,000 pounds = 1 ton (T.)

Units of Time

60 seconds (sec.) = 1 minute (min.)

60 minutes = 1 hour (hr.)

24 hours = 1 day

7 days = 1 week

52 weeks = 1 year (yr.)

12 months = 1 year

365 days = 1 year

*Notice that ounces are used to measure the dimensions of both volume and weight.

Converting Units

When performing mathematical operations, it can be necessary to convert units of measure to simplify a problem. Units of measure are converted by using either multiplication or division.

To convert from a larger unit into a smaller unit, multiply the given number of larger units by the number of smaller units in only one of the larger units:

(given number of the larger units)

× (the number of smaller units per larger unit)

= answer in smaller units.

For example, to find the number of inches in 5 feet, multiply 5, the number of larger units, by 12, the number of inches in one foot:

5 feet = $\underline{\ ?\ }$ inches?

5 feet × 12 (the number of inches in a single foot) = 60 inches: 5 ft. × $\frac{12 \text{ in.}}{1 \text{ ft.}}$ = 60 in.

Therefore, there are 60 inches in 5 feet.

Example

Change 3.5 tons to pounds:

3.5 tons = $\underline{\ ?\ }$ pounds

1. Determine how many pounds equal 1 ton: 2,000 pounds = 1 ton
2. Multiply the given number of larger units by the number of smaller units in only one of the larger units:

    3.5 tons × $\frac{2,000 \text{ pounds}}{1 \text{ ton}}$ = 7,000 pounds

    Therefore, there are 7,000 pounds in 3.5 tons.

To change a smaller unit to a larger unit, divide the given number of smaller units by the number of smaller units in only one of the larger units:

$$\frac{\text{given number of smaller units}}{\text{number of smaller units per larger unit}}$$

= answer in larger units

For example, to find the number of pints in 64 ounces, divide 64, the number of smaller units, by 16, the number of ounces in one pint.

64 ounces = $\underline{\ ?\ }$ pints?

$$\frac{64 \text{ ounces}}{16 \text{ ounces per pint}} = 4 \text{ pints}$$

Therefore, 64 ounces equals four pints.

Example
Change 32 ounces to pounds:

32 ounces = _?_ pounds

1. Determine how many ounces equal 1 pound:
   16 ounces = 1 pound
2. Divide the given number of smaller units by the number of smaller units in only one of the larger units:

   $$\frac{32 \text{ ounces}}{16 \text{ ounces per pound}} = 2 \text{ pounds}$$

   Therefore, 32 ounces equals two pounds.

Practice

Solve the following problems.

1. 6 feet = _____ yards

2. A recipe calls for 3 ounces of olive oil. Convert this measurement into cups.

3. 48 inches = _____ yards

4. A 2-liter bottle of soda contains approximately how many fluid ounces?

5. Martha walks from her apartment to the park, a distance of 0.85 miles. What is the distance she walks to the park in feet?

6. A road race is 33,000 feet long. How many miles long is the race?

7. 4.5 miles = _____ feet

8. Teresa is following the directions for mixing cement. According to the directions, she needs 13 gallons of water for the amount of cement mix she is using. She only has a container that measures liters. If 1 gallon = 3.8 liters, how many liters will she need?

9. Mishka took a water measurement that read 174 milliliters. All his records need to be in liters. Based on the 174 milliliters reading, how many liters should he record?

10. Tess works at a fabric store and is helping a customer who wants to buy 2 yards of French ribbon. If the price of the ribbon is $0.75 per foot, what is the total cost to the customer?

Basic Operations with Measurement

You may need to add, subtract, multiply, and divide with measurement. The mathematical rules needed for each of these operations with measurement follow.

Addition with Measurements
To add measurements, follow these two steps:

1. Add like units.
2. Simplify the answer by converting smaller units into larger units when possible.

Example
Add 4 pounds 5 ounces to 20 ounces.

1. Be sure to add ounces to ounces:

	4 lb.	5 oz.
+		20 oz.
	4 lb.	25 oz.

2. Because 25 ounces is more than 16 ounces (1 pound), simplify by dividing by 16:

$$\begin{array}{r} 1 \text{ lb. R9 oz.} \\ 16 \text{ oz.} \overline{)25 \text{ oz.}} \\ -16 \text{ oz.} \\ \hline 9 \text{ oz.} \end{array}$$

3. Then add the 1 pound to the 4 pounds:
4 pounds 25 ounces = 4 pounds +
1 pound 9 ounces = 5 pounds 9 ounces

Subtraction with Measurements

1. Subtract like units if possible.
2. If not, regroup units to allow for subtraction.
3. Write the answer in simplest form.

For example, 6 pounds 2 ounces subtracted from 9 pounds 10 ounces.

$$\begin{array}{l} 9 \text{ lb. 10 oz.} \\ -6 \text{ lb. } 2 \text{ oz.} \\ \hline 3 \text{ lb. } 8 \text{ oz.} \end{array}$$ Subtract ounces from ounces. Then subtract pounds from pounds.

Sometimes, it is necessary to regroup units when subtracting.

Example

Subtract 3 yards 2 feet from 5 yards 1 foot.

Because 2 feet cannot be taken from 1 foot, regroup 1 yard from the 5 yards and convert the 1 yard to 3 feet. Add 3 feet to 1 foot. Then subtract feet from feet and yards from yards:

$$\begin{array}{l} \overset{4}{\cancel{5}} \text{ yd. } \overset{4}{\cancel{1}} \text{ ft.} \\ -3 \text{ yd. 2 ft.} \\ \hline 1 \text{ yd. 2 ft.} \end{array}$$

5 yards 1 foot − 3 yards 2 feet = 1 yard 2 feet

Multiplication with Measurements

1. Multiply like units if units are involved.
2. Simplify the answer.

Example

Multiply 5 feet 7 inches by 3.

1. Multiply 7 inches by 3, then multiply 5 feet by 3. Keep the units separate:

$$\begin{array}{r} 5 \text{ ft. } 7 \text{ in.} \\ \times \quad 3 \\ \hline 15 \text{ ft. 21 in.} \end{array}$$

2. Since 12 inches = 1 foot, simplify 21 inches:
15 ft. 21 in. = 15 ft. + 1 ft. 9 in. = 16 ft. 9 in.

Example

Multiply 9 feet by 4 yards.

First, decide on a common unit: either change the 9 feet to yards, or change the 4 yards to feet. Both options are explained below:

Option 1:

To change yards to feet, multiply the number of feet in a yard (3) by the number of yards in this problem (4).

3 feet in a yard × 4 yards = 12 feet

Then multiply: 9 feet × 12 feet = 108 square feet.
(Note: feet × feet = square feet = ft.^{2}.)

Option 2:

To change feet to yards, divide the number of feet given (9), by the number of feet in a yard (3).

9 feet ÷ 3 feet in a yard = 3 yards

Then multiply 3 yards by 4 yards =
12 square yards.
(Note: yards × yards = square yards = yd.^{2}.)

Division with Measurements

1. Divide into the larger units first.
2. Convert the remainder to the smaller unit.
3. Add the converted remainder to the existing smaller unit if any.

4. Then divide into smaller units.

5. Write the answer in simplest form.

Example

Divide 5 quarts 4 ounces by 4.

1. Divide into the larger unit:

$$\begin{array}{r} 1 \text{ qt. R1 qt.} \\ 4\overline{)5 \text{ qt.}} \\ \underline{-4 \text{ qt.}} \\ 1 \text{ qt.} \end{array}$$

2. Convert the remainder:
   1 qt. = 32 oz.

3. Add the remainder to the original smaller unit:
   32 oz. + 4 oz. = 36 oz.

4. Divide into smaller units:
   36 oz. ÷ 4 = 9 oz.

5. Write answer in simplest form:
   1 qt. 9 oz.

Practice

Solve the following problems.

11. Thomas is 6 feet 1 inch in height. His son is 3 feet 3 inches tall. What is the difference in their heights, in inches?

12. 2 pints 6 ounces + 1 cup 7 ounces = _____

13. A carpenter is measuring a piece of plywood. The piece of plywood it 8 feet 7 inches long. He only needs a piece of plywood 7 feet 6 inches long. How many inches does he need to cut off to have the correct length?

14. A customer service representative is asked how many miles the company is from Town A. She knows that the company is between Town A and Town B. She also knows that it is 16.6 miles between Town A and Town B, and that Town B is 7.2 miles from the company. What is the correct answer to the customer's question?

15. Horatio is asked by his supervisor to consolidate 3 bins of apples into one. The first bin has 5 pounds 6 ounces of apples, the second has 7 pounds 12 ounces, and the third has 14 pounds 4 ounces. After he puts all the apples into one bin, what is the total weight of the apples? (1 pound = 16 ounces)

Metric Measurements

The metric system is an international system of measurement also called the decimal system. Converting units in the metric system is much easier than converting units in the English system of measurement. However, making conversions between the two systems is much more difficult. The basic units of the metric system are the meter, gram, and liter. Here is a general idea of how the two systems compare:

Metric System	English System
1 meter	A meter is a little more than a yard; it is equal to about 39 inches
1 gram	A gram is a very small unit of weight; there are about 30 grams in one ounce.
1 liter	A liter is a little more than a quart.

Prefixes are attached to the basic metric units listed above to indicate the amount of each unit.

For example, the prefix *deci* means one-tenth ($\frac{1}{10}$); therefore, one decigram is one-tenth of a gram, and one decimeter is one-tenth of a meter. The following six prefixes can be used with every metric unit:

KILO	HECTO	DEKA	DECI	CENTI	MILLI
(k)	(h)	(dk)	(d)	(c)	(m)
1,000	100	10	$\frac{1}{10}$	$\frac{1}{100}$	$\frac{1}{1,000}$

Examples

- 1 hectometer = 1 hm = 100 meters
- 1 millimeter = 1 mm = $\frac{1}{1,000}$ meter = .001 meter
- 1 dekagram = 1 dkg = 10 grams
- 1 centiliter = 1 cL* = $\frac{1}{100}$ liter = .01 liter
- 1 kilogram = 1 kg = 1,000 grams
- 1 deciliter = 1 dL* = $\frac{1}{10}$ liter = .1 liter

*Notice that liter is abbreviated with a capital letter—"L."

This table illustrates some common relationships used in the metric system.

LENGTH	WEIGHT	VOLUME
1 km = 1,000 m	1 kg = 1,000 g	1 kL = 1,000 L
1 m = .001 km	1 g = .001 kg	1 L = .001 kL
1 m = 100 cm	1 g = 100 cg	1 L = 100 cL
1 cm = .01 m	1 cg = .01 g	1 cL = .01 L
1 m = 1,000 mm	1 g = 1,000 mg	1 L = 1,000 mL
1 mm = .001 m	1 mg = .001 g	1 mL = .001 L

Conversions within the Metric System

An easy way to do conversions with the metric system is to move the decimal point either to the right or left because the conversion factor is always ten or a power of ten. Remember, when changing from a large unit to a smaller unit, multiply. When changing from a small unit to a larger unit, divide.

Making Easy Conversions within the Metric System

When multiplying by a power of ten, move the decimal point to the right, since the number becomes larger. When dividing by a power of ten, move the decimal point to the left, since the number becomes smaller.

To change from a large unit to a smaller unit, move the decimal point to the right.

$$\rightarrow$$
kilo hecto deka UNIT deci centi milli
$$\leftarrow$$

To change from a small unit to a larger unit, move the decimal point to the left.

Example

Change 520 grams to kilograms.

1. Be aware that changing meters to kilometers is going from small units to larger units and, thus, requires that the decimal point move to the left.
2. Beginning at the UNIT (for grams), note that the Kilo heading is three places away. Therefore, the decimal point will move three places to the left.
3. Move the decimal point from the end of 520 to the left three places. Place the decimal point before the 5.
   520 ←
   .520

The answer is 520 grams = .520 kilograms.

Example

Ron's supply truck can hold a total of 20,000 kilograms. If he exceeds that limit, he must buy stabilizers for the truck that cost $12.80 each. Each stabilizer can hold 100 additional kilograms. If he wants to pack 22,300,000 grams of supplies, how much money will he have to spend on the stabilizers?

1. First, change 2,300,000 grams to kilograms. Move the decimal point 3 places to the left:
   22,300,000 g = 22,300.000 kg = 22,300 kg

2. Subtract to find the amount over the limit:
   22,300 kg − 20,000 kg = 2,300 kg

3. Because each stabilizer holds 100 kilograms and the supplies exceed the weight limit of the truck by 2,300 kilograms, Ron must purchase 23 stabilizers:
   2,300 kg ÷ 100 kg per stabilizer = 23 stabilizers.

4. Each stabilizer costs $12.80, so multiply $12.80 by 23:
   $12.80 × 23 = $294.40

Practice

Solve the following metric problems.

16. Edmund is doing repairs on a house and needs to cut a square in the wall for an intercom. Each side of the square needs to be 18 cm. If 1 inch = 2.54 centimeters, how many inches is each side? (Round to the tenths place.)

17. An electrician needs to calculate how many centimeters of electrical tape he needs for a job. If there are 100 centimeters in 1 meter, how many centimeters of electrical tape will he need if he needs 10 meters of tape?

18. A telemarketer is arranging the delivery of a large piece of exercise equipment to a customer. The moving company charges $0.40 per pound and $0.35 per mile. The exercise machine weighs 215 pounds and the customer lives 88 kilometers away. How much will the cost of delivery be? (1 mile = 1.6 kilometers.)

Answers

1. 2 yds.
2. 0.375 c.
3. $1\frac{1}{3}$ yd.
4. 486.4 oz.
5. 4,488 ft.
6. 6.25 mi.
7. 23,760 ft.
8. 49.4 L
9. 0.174 L
10. $4.50
11. 34 in.
12. 3 pt. 5 oz.
13. 13 in.
14. 9.4 mi.
15. 27 lb. 6 oz.
16. 7.0866 ≈ 7.1 in.
17. 1,000 cm.
18. $105.25

11 ▶ Geometry Review

This chapter familiarizes you with the properties of angles, lines, polygons, triangles, and circles, as well as the formulas for area, volume, and perimeter.

Geometry is the study of shapes and the relationships among them. The geometry that is necessary to function in the workforce is fundamental and practical. Basic concepts in geometry will be detailed and applied in this section. The study of geometry always begins with a look at basic vocabulary and concepts. Therefore, a list of definitions and important formulas is provided here.

GEOMETRY TERMS

Area	The space inside a 2-dimensional figure
Circumference	The distance around a circle
Chord	A line segment that goes through a circle, with its endpoints on the circle
Diameter	A chord that goes directly through the center of a circle—the longest line that can be drawn in a circle
Hypotenuse	The longest leg of a right triangle, always opposite the right angle
Leg	Either of the two sides of a right triangle that make the right angle
Perimeter	The distance around a figure
Radius	A line from the center of a circle to a point on the circle (half of the diameter)
Surface Area	The sum of the areas of all of a 3-dimensional figure's faces
Volume	The space inside a 3-dimensional figure

GEOMETRY FORMULAS

Perimeter	The sum of all the sides of a figure
Circumference	$2\pi r$, or πd
Area of a rectangle	$A = bh$
Area of a triangle	$A = \frac{1}{2}bh$

Note: It is important to remember that the height of a triangle is not necessarily one of the sides of the triangle. The height will always be associated with a line (called an altitude) that comes from one vertex (angle) to the opposite side and forms a right angle (signified by the box). In other words, the height must always be perpendicular to (form a right angle with) the base.

Area of a circle	$A = \pi r^2$
Volume of a cylindrical solid	$A = \pi r^2 h$
Volume of a rectangular solid	$V = lwh$

Key:
π = a ratio used for circles. Most of the time it is okay to approximate π with 3.14. Most calculators have a π key.
r = radius of a circle
d = diameter of a circle
b = base of a figure, primarily for triangles and rectangles
h = height of a figure
l = length of a figure
w = width of a figure, primarily for rectangular objects

Geometry questions often assume that you know the number of sides for different shapes. This list shows the relationship between shapes and the number of sides.

SHAPE	NUMBER OF SIDES
Circle	0
Triangle	3
Quadrilateral (square/rectangle)	4
Pentagon	5
Hexagon	6
Heptagon	7
Octagon	8
Nonagon	9
Decagon	10

Practice

Answer the following questions.

1. A bag of concrete mix makes 15 cubic feet of concrete. How many bags of concrete mix need to be purchased to fill a walkway that is 50 cubic feet?

2. The perimeter of a rectangular garden is 50 feet. Find the width of the garden if the length is 15 feet.

3. A farmer has 24 feet of fencing. She wants to create the animal pen with the greatest possible area using exactly 24 feet of fencing. Which of the following dimensions would create the pen with the greatest area and use exactly 24 feet of fencing?
   a. 6 feet by 6 feet
   b. 8 feet by 4 feet
   c. 2 feet by 10 feet
   d. 10 feet by 14 feet

4. A slab of concrete is needed on the third floor of a building. The contractor must calculate the weight of the concrete to ensure that the building will be structurally sound. The concrete slab will be 10 feet by 12 feet and 2 feet thick. The concrete weighs 95 pounds per cubic foot. What is the weight of the concrete slab? (Volume = length × width × height)

5. A painter must paint a room that measures 12 feet by 15 feet. The ceiling of the room is 8 feet high. Each gallon of paint costs $25.50 and covers 300 square feet of wall. How much will the paint cost him assuming that the painter will only paint one coat on each wall?

6. A circular compact disc has a diameter of 12 cm and a height of 2 mm. If Kerry stacks 10 compact discs on top of each other, what is the volume of the stack?

Angles

An angle is formed by an endpoint, or vertex, and two rays. A ray includes an endpoint and a line shooting off into one direction.

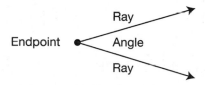

Classifying Angles

Angles can be classified into the following categories: acute, right, obtuse, and straight.

- An acute angle is an angle that measures between 0 and 90 degrees.

Acute Angle

- A right angle is an angle that measures exactly 90 degrees. A right angle is symbolized by a square at the vertex.

Right Angle

- An obtuse angle is an angle that measures more than 90 degrees, but less than 180 degrees.

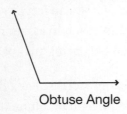

Obtuse Angle

- A straight angle is an angle that measures 180 degrees. Thus, both of its sides form a line.

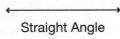

Straight Angle

Complementary Angles

Two angles are complementary if the sum of their measures is equal to 90 degrees.

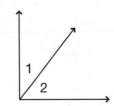

Complementary Angles

Supplementary Angles

Two angles are supplementary if the sum of their measures is equal to 180 degrees.

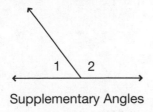

Supplementary Angles

Practice

Use the following diagram to answer questions 7 through 11. The diagram is not to scale.

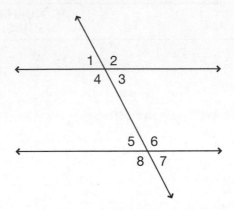

7. If the measure of angle 2 is equal to $12x + 10$ and the measure of angle 8 is equal to $7x - 1$, what is the measure of angle 2?

8. If the measure of angle 5 is five times the measure of angle 6, what is the measure of angle 5?

9. If the measure of angle 4 is $6x + 20$ and the measure of angle 7 is $10x - 40$, what is the measure of angle 6?

10. Which of the following is NOT true if the measure of angle 3 is 90°?
   a. Angles 1 and 2 are complementary.
   b. Angles 3 and 6 are supplementary.
   c. Angles 5 and 7 are adjacent.
   d. Angles 5 and 7 are congruent.
   e. Angles 4 and 8 are supplementary and congruent.

11. If the measure of angle 2 is $8x + 10$ and the measure of angle 6 is $x2 - 38$, what is the measure of angle 8?

Angles of a Triangle

The sum of the measures of the three angles in a triangle always equals 180 degrees.

Exterior Angles

An exterior angle can be formed by extending a side from any of the three vertices of a triangle. Here are some rules for working with exterior angles:

- An exterior angle and an interior angle that share the same vertex are supplementary. In other words, exterior angles and interior angles form straight lines with each other.
- An exterior angle is equal to the sum of the non-adjacent interior angles.
- The sum of the exterior angles of a triangle equals 360 degrees.

Example

In the following diagram, sides *AC* and *AB* of triangle *ABC* are congruent. If the measure of angle *DCA* is 115 degrees, what is the measure in degrees of angle *A*?

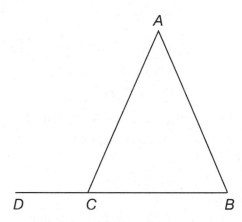

1. Angles *DCA* and *ACB* form a line; therefore, the measures of these angles add to 180°: 180 − *DCA* = *ACB*, 180 − 115 = 65°
2. Since sides *AC* and *AB* are congruent, triangle *ABC* is isosceles. The angles opposite the congruent sides are congruent. Therefore, angle *ABC* is also 65°.
3. Since there are 180° in a triangle, the measure of angle A = 180 − 65 − 65 = 50°.

Classifying Triangles

It is possible to classify triangles into three categories based on the number of equal sides:

SCALENE TRIANGLE	ISOSCELES TRIANGLE	EQUILATERAL TRIANGLE
no equal sides)	≥ two equal sides	all sides equal

It is also possible to classify triangles into three categories based on the measure of the greatest angle:

ACUTE TRIANGLE	RIGHT TRIANGLE	OBTUSE TRIANGLE
greatest angle is acute	greatest angle is 90°	greatest angle is obtuse

Angle-Side Relationships

Knowing the angle-side relationships in isosceles, equilateral, and right triangles may be helpful in work-related situations.

- In isosceles triangles, equal angles are opposite equal sides.

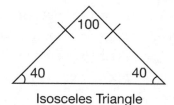

Isosceles Triangle

- In equilateral triangles, all sides are equal and all angles are equal. The measure of the angles in an equilateral triangle is always 60 degrees.

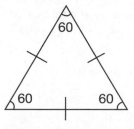

Equilateral Triangle

- In a right triangle, the side opposite the right angle is called the hypotenuse and the other sides are called legs. The box in the angle of the 90-degree angle symbolizes that the triangle is in fact a right triangle.

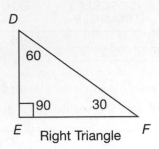

Right Triangle

Practice

Answer the following questions.

12. If the measure of angle A of triangle ABC is $3x$, the measure of angle B is $5x$, and the measure of angle C is $4x$, what is the value of x?

13. If the measure of angle A of triangle ABC is $5x + 10$, the measure of angle B is $x + 10$, and the measure of angle C is $2x$, which of the following is true of triangle ABC?
   a. Triangle ABC is acute and scalene.
   b. Triangle ABC is acute but not scalene.
   c. Triangle ABC is right but not isosceles.
   d. Triangle ABC is obtuse but not scalene.
   e. Triangle ABC is obtuse and scalene.

14. The measure of an angle exterior to angle F of triangle DEF measures $16x + 12$. If angle F measures $8x$, what is the measure of angle F?

15. If the measures of angles A and B of triangle ABC are each $2x + 5$ and the measure of angle C is $3x - 5$, what is the measure of the angle exterior to angle A?

16. The measure of an angle exterior to angle F of triangle DEF measures 120°. Which of the following must be true?
   a. Triangle DEF is obtuse.
   b. Triangle DEF is acute.
   c. Triangle DEF is equilateral.
   d. Triangle DEF is scalene.
   e. Triangle DEF is not isosceles.

Pythagorean Theorem

The **Pythagorean theorem** is an important tool for working with right triangles.

It states: $a^2 + b^2 = c^2$, where a and b represent the legs and c represents the hypotenuse.

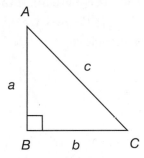

This theorem makes it easy to find the length of any side as along as the measure of two sides is known.

Example
If leg $a = 1$ and leg $b = 2$ in a triangle, find the measure of the hypotenuse, c.
$$a^2 + b^2 = c^2$$
$$1^2 + 2^2 = c^2$$
$$1 + 4 = c^2$$
$$5 = c^2$$
$$\sqrt{5} = c$$

Comparing Triangles

Triangles are said to be congruent (indicated by the symbol ≅) when they have exactly the same size and shape. Two triangles are congruent if their corresponding parts (their angles and sides) are congruent. Sometimes, it is easy to tell if two triangles are congruent by looking. However, in geometry, it must be able to be proven that the triangles are congruent.

If two triangles are congruent, one of the three criteria listed below must be satisfied.

Side-Side-Side (SSS)	The side measures for both triangles are the same.
Side-Angle-Side (SAS)	Two sides and the angle between them are the same.
Angle-Side-Angle (ASA)	Two angles and the side between them are the same.

Polygons

Polygons are closed figures with three or more sides, for example triangles, rectangles, and pentagons.

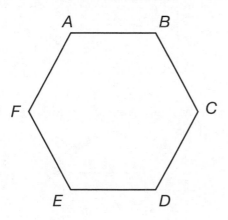

Terms Related to Polygons

- Vertices are corner points, also called endpoints, of a polygon. The vertices in the preceding polygon are: A, B, C, D, E, and F and they are always labeled with capital letters.
- A regular polygon has sides and angles that are all equal.
- An equiangular polygon has angles that are all equal.

Angles of a Quadrilateral

A quadrilateral is a four-sided polygon. Since a quadrilateral can be divided by a diagonal into two triangles, the sum of its interior angles will equal 180 + 180 = 360 degrees.

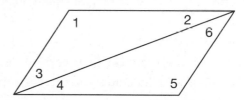

$$m\angle 1 + m\angle 2 + m\angle 3 + m\angle 4 + m\angle 5 + m\angle 6 = 360°$$

Interior Angles

To find the sum of the interior angles of any polygon, use this formula:

$S = 180(x - 2)°$, where x = the number of sides of the polygon.

Example
Find the sum of the interior angles in the polygon.

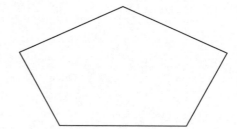

The polygon is a pentagon that has 5 sides, so substitute 5 for x in the formula:

$$S = (5 - 2) \times 180°$$
$$S = 3 \times 180°$$
$$S = 540°$$

Practice

17. Steve draws a polygon with 12 sides. What is the sum of the measures of the interior angles of Steve's polygon?

Exterior Angles

Similar to the exterior angles of a triangle, the sum of the exterior angles of any polygon equals 360 degrees.

Similar Polygons

If two polygons are similar, their corresponding angles are equal and the ratios of the corresponding sides are in proportion.

Example

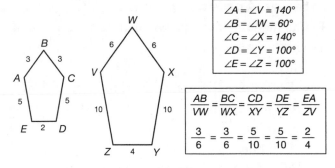

$\angle A = \angle V = 140°$	
$\angle B = \angle W = 60°$	
$\angle C = \angle X = 140°$	
$\angle D = \angle Y = 100°$	
$\angle E = \angle Z = 100°$	

$$\frac{AB}{VW} = \frac{BC}{WX} = \frac{CD}{XY} = \frac{DE}{YZ} = \frac{EA}{ZV}$$

$$\frac{3}{6} = \frac{3}{6} = \frac{5}{10} = \frac{5}{10} = \frac{2}{4}$$

These two polygons are similar because their angles are equal and the ratios of the corresponding sides are in proportion.

Parallelograms

A parallelogram is a quadrilateral with two pairs of parallel sides.

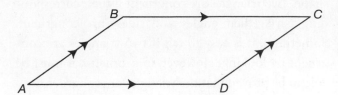

In the figure, $\overline{AB} \parallel \overline{CD}$ and $\overline{BC} \parallel \overline{AD}$. Parallel lines are symbolized with matching numbers of triangles or arrows.

A parallelogram has:

- opposite sides that are equal ($AB = CD$ and $BC = AD$)
- opposite angles that are equal (m$\angle A$ = m$\angle C$ and m$\angle B$ = m$\angle D$)
- consecutive angles that are supplementary (m$\angle A$ + m$\angle B$ = 180°, m$\angle B$ + m$\angle C$ = 180°, m$\angle C$ + m$\angle D$ = 180°, m$\angle D$ + m$\angle A$ = 180°)

Special Types of Parallelograms

- A rectangle is a parallelogram that has four right angles.

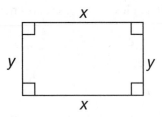

- A rhombus is a parallelogram that has four equal sides.

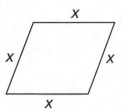

- A square is a parallelogram in which all angles are equal to 90 degrees and all sides are equal to each other. A square is a special case of a rectangle where all the sides are equal. A square is also a special type of rhombus where all the angles are equal.

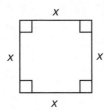

Example

Which of the following statements is true?

  a. All squares are rectangles and rhombuses.

  b. All rectangles are rhombuses, but not all rhombuses are rectangles.

  c. All rhombuses are parallelograms and all parallelograms are rhombuses.

  d. All rhombuses are squares, but not all squares are rhombuses.

  e. All squares are parallelograms, but not all squares are rectangles.

Only statement **a** is true. A parallelogram is a quadrilateral with two pairs of parallel sides. All rectangles, rhombuses, and squares are parallelograms. A rectangle is a parallelogram with four right angles. All rectangles are parallelograms, but not all parallelograms are rectangles. A rhombus is a parallelogram with four equal sides. All rhombuses are parallelograms, but not all rhombuses are rectangles and not all parallelograms are rhombuses. A square is a parallelogram with four right angles and four equal sides. All squares are rectangles, rhombuses, and parallelograms, but not all rectangles are squares, not all rhombuses are squares, and not all parallelograms are squares.

Practice

18. If *ABCD* (shown here) is a parallelogram, what is the measure of angle *ABC*?

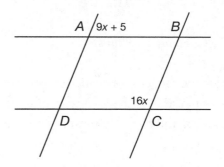

Circles

Remember the following facts about circles:

- A circle contains 360 degrees.
- The midpoint of a circle is called the center.
- The distance around a circle is called the circumference
- The line segment that goes through a circle, with its endpoints on the circle, is called a chord.
- A chord that goes directly through the center of a circle—the longest line that can be drawn in a circle—is called the diameter
- The line from the center of a circle to a point on the circle (half of the diameter) is called the radius.
- The area of a circle is $A = \pi r^2$
- The circumference of a circle is $2\pi r$, or πd.

Example

A circle has an area of 64π ft^2. What is the circumference of the circle?

  1. The area of a circle is equal to πr^2, where r is the radius of the circle. Find what times itself equals 64:

    $8 \times 8 = 64$

    Therefore, the radius of this circle is equal to 8 ft.

2. The circumference of a circle is equal to $2\pi r$. Substitute the known radius: $2\pi(8) = 16\pi$ ft.

Practice

Answer the following questions.

19. How much fencing is needed to enclose a circular garden with a diameter of 12 feet? Use 3.14 for π and round your answer to the next whole foot.

20. How many cubic feet of concrete are needed to form a circular column 7 feet high with a diameter of 3 feet? (Volume $= \pi r^2 h$. Use 3.14 for π and round your answer to the next cubic foot.)

Answers

1. 4 bags need to be purchased.

2. The two widths are each 10 feet.

3. Choice **a**, a 6-foot by 6-foot pen, has the greatest area.

4. 22,800 pounds

5. $51.00

6. 72π cm^3

7. 118°

8. 150°

9. 110°

10. a. If angle 3 measures 90°, then angles 1, 6, and 7 must also measure 90°, since they are alternating angles. Angles 3 and 4 are supplementary, since these angles form a line. Therefore, the measure of angle 4 is equal to 180 − 90 = 90°. Angles 3 and 4 are congruent and supplementary. Since angles 2, 4, 5, and 8 are alternating angles, they are all congruent to each other. Every numbered angle measures 90°. Therefore, every numbered angle is congruent and supplementary to every other numbered angle.

Angles 5 and 7 are in fact adjacent, since they share a common vertex and a common ray.

However, angles 1 and 2 are not complementary—their measures add to 180°, not 90°.

11. 74°

12. $x = 15$

13. e. The measures of the angles of a triangle add to 180°. Therefore, $5x + 10 + x + 10 + 2x = 180$, $8x + 20 = 180$, $8x = 160$, and $x = 20$. The measure of angle A is $5(20) + 10 = 110$, the measure of angle B is $(20) + 10 = 30$, and the measure of angle C is $2(20) = 40$. Since the largest angle of triangle ABC is greater than 90° and no two angles of the triangle are equal in measure, triangle ABC is obtuse and scalene.

14. 56°

15. 125°

16. e. Since an angle exterior to angle F is 120°, the measure of interior angle F is 60°, and the sum of the measures of interior angles D and E is 120°. Angles D and E could each measure 60°, making triangle DEF acute and equilateral, but these angles could also measure 100° and 20° respectively, making triangle DEF obtuse and scalene. However, triangle DEF cannot be isosceles. Angle F measures 60°; if either angles D or E measure 60°, the other must also measure 60°, making triangle DEF equilateral. Angles D and E cannot be congruent to each other without also being congruent to angle F. Therefore, triangle DEF can be acute, obtuse, scalene, or equilateral, but not isosceles.

17. 1,800

18. 68°

19. 38 feet

20. 50 cubic feet

On this practice exam, you will encounter 80 questions covering the topics you have studied in Chapters 4 through 10. You should have a pencil and scrap paper handy; however, do not use a calculator.

It is not necessary to take this practice exam under timed conditions. If you choose to time yourself, however, allow about 40 minutes to complete this practice exam.

When you are finished, check the answer key on page 150 carefully to assess your results. Good luck!

1.	(a)	(b)	(c)	(d)
2.	(a)	(b)	(c)	(d)
3.	(a)	(b)	(c)	(d)
4.	(a)	(b)	(c)	(d)
5.	(a)	(b)	(c)	(d)
6.	(a)	(b)	(c)	(d)
7.	(a)	(b)	(c)	(d)
8.	(a)	(b)	(c)	(d)
9.	(a)	(b)	(c)	(d)
10.	(a)	(b)	(c)	(d)
11.	(a)	(b)	(c)	(d)
12.	(a)	(b)	(c)	(d)
13.	(a)	(b)	(c)	(d)
14.	(a)	(b)	(c)	(d)
15.	(a)	(b)	(c)	(d)
16.	(a)	(b)	(c)	(d)
17.	(a)	(b)	(c)	(d)
18.	(a)	(b)	(c)	(d)
19.	(a)	(b)	(c)	(d)
20.	(a)	(b)	(c)	(d)
21.	(a)	(b)	(c)	(d)
22.	(a)	(b)	(c)	(d)
23.	(a)	(b)	(c)	(d)
24.	(a)	(b)	(c)	(d)
25.	(a)	(b)	(c)	(d)
26.	(a)	(b)	(c)	(d)
27.	(a)	(b)	(c)	(d)

28.	(a)	(b)	(c)	(d)
29.	(a)	(b)	(c)	(d)
30.	(a)	(b)	(c)	(d)
31.	(a)	(b)	(c)	(d)
32.	(a)	(b)	(c)	(d)
33.	(a)	(b)	(c)	(d)
34.	(a)	(b)	(c)	(d)
35.	(a)	(b)	(c)	(d)
36.	(a)	(b)	(c)	(d)
37.	(a)	(b)	(c)	(d)
38.	(a)	(b)	(c)	(d)
39.	(a)	(b)	(c)	(d)
40.	(a)	(b)	(c)	(d)
41.	(a)	(b)	(c)	(d)
42.	(a)	(b)	(c)	(d)
43.	(a)	(b)	(c)	(d)
44.	(a)	(b)	(c)	(d)
45.	(a)	(b)	(c)	(d)
46.	(a)	(b)	(c)	(d)
47.	(a)	(b)	(c)	(d)
48.	(a)	(b)	(c)	(d)
49.	(a)	(b)	(c)	(d)
50.	(a)	(b)	(c)	(d)
51.	(a)	(b)	(c)	(d)
52.	(a)	(b)	(c)	(d)
53.	(a)	(b)	(c)	(d)
54.	(a)	(b)	(c)	(d)

55.	(a)	(b)	(c)	(d)
56.	(a)	(b)	(c)	(d)
57.	(a)	(b)	(c)	(d)
58.	(a)	(b)	(c)	(d)
59.	(a)	(b)	(c)	(d)
60.	(a)	(b)	(c)	(d)
61.	(a)	(b)	(c)	(d)
62.	(a)	(b)	(c)	(d)
63.	(a)	(b)	(c)	(d)
64.	(a)	(b)	(c)	(d)
65.	(a)	(b)	(c)	(d)
66.	(a)	(b)	(c)	(d)
67.	(a)	(b)	(c)	(d)
68.	(a)	(b)	(c)	(d)
69.	(a)	(b)	(c)	(d)
70.	(a)	(b)	(c)	(d)
71.	(a)	(b)	(c)	(d)
72.	(a)	(b)	(c)	(d)
73.	(a)	(b)	(c)	(d)
74.	(a)	(b)	(c)	(d)
75.	(a)	(b)	(c)	(d)
76.	(a)	(b)	(c)	(d)
77.	(a)	(b)	(c)	(d)
78.	(a)	(b)	(c)	(d)
79.	(a)	(b)	(c)	(d)
80.	(a)	(b)	(c)	(d)

1. What is the positive difference between 10,752
and 675?
   a. 11,427
   b. 10,077
   c. 3,822
   d. −10,077

2. What is the product of 523 and 13 when
rounded to the nearest hundred?
   a. 6,799
   b. 536
   c. 6,800
   d. 500

3. What is the sum of the product of 3 and 2 and
the product of 4 and 5?
   a. 14
   b. 26
   c. 45
   d. 120

4. $582 - 73 =$
   a. 42,486
   b. 655
   c. 519
   d. 509

5. Solve the following:
$589 + 7,995 \div 15 =$
   a. 572 with a remainder of 4
   b. 1,122
   c. 8,569
   d. 8,599

6. $540 \div 6 + 3 \times 24 =$
   a. 2,232
   b. 1,440
   c. 1,260
   d. 162

7. $(8^3)^5 =$
   a. 8^{15}
   b. 8^8
   c. 8^4
   d. 8^2

8. $7^3 =$
   a. 343
   b. 49
   c. 38
   d. 21

9. Which of the following expressions is the
prime factorization of 60?
   a. 2×30
   b. $2 \times 2 \times 4 \times 5$
   c. 10×6
   d. $2 \times 2 \times 3 \times 5$

10. Which of the following numbers is NOT a
factor of 36?
   a. 6
   b. 12
   c. 2
   d. 13

11. $9\frac{3}{7} + 4\frac{2}{5} =$
   a. $13\frac{5}{12}$
   b. $13\frac{3}{4}$
   c. $13\frac{29}{35}$
   d. $13\frac{27}{52}$

12. $\frac{5}{6} + \frac{3}{8} =$
   a. $\frac{8}{14}$
   b. $\frac{2}{14}$
   c. $\frac{11}{24}$
   d. $1\frac{5}{24}$

13. $43\frac{2}{3} + 20\frac{2}{9} =$
   a. $63\frac{8}{9}$
   b. $63\frac{7}{9}$
   c. $63\frac{4}{9}$
   d. $63\frac{4}{12}$

14. $\frac{7}{8} - \frac{3}{5} =$
- **a.** $\frac{11}{40}$
- **b.** $1\frac{1}{3}$
- **c.** $\frac{1}{10}$
- **d.** $1\frac{19}{40}$

15. $\frac{4}{7} - \frac{1}{3} =$
- **a.** $\frac{5}{10}$
- **b.** $\frac{3}{4}$
- **c.** $\frac{4}{21}$
- **d.** $\frac{5}{21}$

16. $-\frac{5}{3} - \frac{1}{3} =$
- **a.** $\frac{4}{3}$
- **b.** $-\frac{4}{3}$
- **c.** 2
- **d.** -2

17. $\frac{7}{9} \times \frac{9}{7} =$
- **a.** 1
- **b.** $1\frac{1}{9}$
- **c.** $\frac{1}{63}$
- **d.** $\frac{1}{9}$

18. $\frac{5}{12} \times \frac{1}{6} \times \frac{2}{3} =$
- **a.** $\frac{10}{12}$
- **b.** $\frac{8}{21}$
- **c.** $\frac{5}{108}$
- **d.** $\frac{5}{216}$

19. $\frac{7}{9} \times \frac{4}{5} =$
- **a.** $\frac{28}{45}$
- **b.** $\frac{11}{14}$
- **c.** $\frac{35}{36}$
- **d.** $\frac{3}{4}$

20. $\frac{1}{3} \div \frac{2}{7} =$
- **a.** $2\frac{4}{5}$
- **b.** $1\frac{1}{6}$
- **c.** $2\frac{1}{7}$
- **d.** $1\frac{1}{5}$

21. Which of the following numbers has a 3 in the hundredths place?
- **a.** 354.01
- **b.** 0.54031
- **c.** 0.54301
- **d.** 0.03514

22. What is 25.682 rounded to the nearest tenth?
- **a.** 26
- **b.** 25.6
- **c.** 25.68
- **d.** 25.7

23. Which decimal is equivalent to the fraction $\frac{7}{25}$?
- **a.** 0.07
- **b.** 0.35
- **c.** 0.28
- **d.** 0.725

24. What is the sum of 6.76014 and 2.523?
- **a.** 4.23714
- **b.** 8.76014
- **c.** 9.28314
- **d.** 92.8314

25. $14.02 + 0.987 + 0.145 =$
- **a.** 14.152
- **b.** 15.152
- **c.** 14.142
- **d.** 15.142

26. $324.0073 - 87.663 =$
- **a.** 411.6703
- **b.** 237.3443
- **c.** 236.3443
- **d.** 23.634443

27. $8.3 - 1.725 =$
- **a.** 6.575
- **b.** 6.775
- **c.** 7.575
- **d.** 10.025

28. $0.88 \times 0.22 =$
   a. 0.01936
   b. 0.1936
   c. 0.1616
   d. 1.616

29. $0.125 \times 8 \times 0.32 =$
   a. $\frac{32}{1}$
   b. $\frac{1}{10}$
   c. $\frac{8}{250}$
   d. $\frac{32}{100}$

30. $512 \div 0.256 =$
   a. 20
   b. 2,000
   c. 200
   d. 2

31. A fire department consists of 96 full-time and volunteer members. If the ratio of full-time to volunteer members was 2:14, how many full-time members are part of the department?
   a. 14
   b. 16
   c. 28
   d. 84

32. There were 28 people at last week's staff meeting. If the ratio of men to women was 4:3, how many women were at the staff meeting?
   a. 16
   b. 12
   c. 7
   d. 4

33. At a certain corporation, the ratio of clerical workers to executives is 7 to 2. If a combined total of 81 clerical workers and executives work for that corporation, how many clerical workers are there?
   a. 63
   b. 14
   c. 18
   d. 36

34. The Republican-Democratic ratio of a city council committee is equal to the Republican-Democratic ratio of the entire city council. There are 34 Republican and 51 Democrats in the city council. If there are 4 Republicans on the committee, how many Democrats are on the committee?
   a. 2
   b. 3
   c. 4
   d. 6

35. A unit price is a ratio that compares the price of an item to its unit of measurement. To determine which product is the better buy, calculate each one's unit price. Which of these five boxes of Klean-O Detergent is the best buy?
   a. Travel-size: $1 for 5 ounces
   b. Small: $2 for 11 ounces
   c. Regular: $4 for 22 ounces
   d. Large: $7 for 40 ounces

36. Another way to write 26.5% is:
   a. $\frac{0.265}{100}$
   b. $\frac{26}{80}$
   c. $\frac{53}{200}$
   d. $\frac{26.5}{1,000}$

37. 0.037% is equivalent to which of the following fractions?

  a. $\frac{37}{100}$

  b. $\frac{37}{1,000}$

  c. $\frac{37}{10,000}$

  d. $\frac{37}{100,000}$

38. Which of the following is 17% of 6,800?

  a. 115,600

  b. 340

  c. 578

  d. 1,156

39. What percent of $\frac{8}{9}$ is $\frac{2}{3}$?

  a. 33%

  b. 66%

  c. 75%

  d. 133%

40. 36 is what percent of 9?

  a. 0.25%

  b. 4%

  c. 324%

  d. 400%

41. The purchaser for the clothing department of a major retailer can purchase 120 women's sweaters at a cost of $900. What is the cost per sweater?

  a. $1,020.00

  b. $13.00

  c. $7.50

  d. $8.00

42. Two pipes are being used to fill a pool. One fills the pool at the rate of 5 gallons per minute. The other works at the rate of 6 gallons per minute. How long will the pipes take to fill a 6,000-gallon pool if they are used together? Round your answer to the nearest minute.

  a. 500 minutes

  b. 545 minutes

  c. 1,000 minutes

  d. 1,200 minutes

43. If a worker gets paid $15.50/hour working construction and works a 10-hour day, about how much money can he expect to make working during one day?

  a. $124.00

  b. $150.00

  c. $155.00

  d. $1,550.00

44. A housecleaner has run out of window cleaning fluid and wishes to purchase more. At the store, she finds that a 44-ounce bottle of cleaner costs $2.75 while a 55-ounce bottle of a different brand costs $3.70. Which is the better buy?

  a. the 44 ounce bottle

  b. the 55 ounce bottle

  c. The costs are the same per unit.

  d. The answer cannot be determined from the information provided.

45. Joe needs to deliver a washing machine across town. The company truck can travel 65 mph on the highway, which comprises 13 miles of his trip. For the remaining 12 miles, Joe will average 24 mph. Assuming he does not hit traffic, at what time must Joe leave the warehouse in order to arrive at his destination by 1:30 P.M.?
 a. 1:00 P.M.
 b. 12:55 P.M.
 c. 12:50 P.M.
 d. 12:48 P.M.

46. Whiz-Bang Construction can construct a 1,400 square foot home for $20,000. Smithco Building can construct a 2,200 square foot home for $28,000. DJK Builders can construct a 2,500 square foot home for $35,000. If a contractor is looking for a construction company to construct 2,800 square foot homes in a new subdivision, and uses the most economical of the three construction companies, approximately how much will the construction of each home in the subdivision cost? Round the answer to the nearest thousand dollars.
 a. $36,000
 b. $35,000
 c. $40,000
 d. $39,000

47. A cleaning service pays an employee $90 for a particular job. If the employee earns $15 per hour, how many hours did she work?
 a. 5 hours
 b. 5.5 hours
 c. 6 hours
 d. 10 hours

48. A landscape designer purchases 12 flowers for $7.45 each. What is his total bill without tax?
 a. $84.40
 b. $89.40
 c. $90.35
 d. $92.35

49. A customer hands a cashier $20 for a purchase total of $14.52. How much change is due back to the customer?
 a. $5.48
 b. $5.58
 c. $6.48
 d. $6.58

50. A state's sales tax is 7.15%. What is the total cost for a purchase that costs $20 pre-tax?
 a. $1.43
 b. $21.43
 c. $22.53
 d. $26.33

51. This chart gives the times that four swimmers had in their race. Which swimmer had the fastest time?

SWIMMER	TIME (SEC)
Molly	38.51
Jeff	39.23
Asta	37.95
Risa	37.89

 a. Molly
 b. Jeff
 c. Asta
 d. Risa

The following pie chart shows the Johnson family's monthly budget. Use this information to answer questions 52 through 54.

Johnson Family Budget

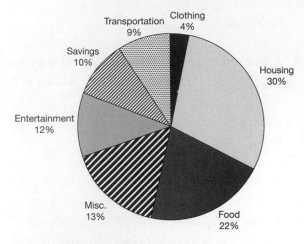

52. In percent of overall expenses, how much more money is spent on food than on transportation and clothing combined?
    a. 9%
    b. 11%
    c. 13%
    d. 22%

53. If the Johnson family budget is $4,000 per month, how much money is spent on housing each month?
    a. $800
    b. $1,000
    c. $1,200
    d. $1,400

54. If the Johnson family budget is $4,000 per month, how much money will they save each year?
    a. $48,000
    b. $4,800
    c. $400
    d. none of the above

The following table shows the numbers of male and female students involved in several types of martial arts. Use this information to answer questions 55 through 57.

ACTIVITY	MALE	FEMALE
Judo	11	13
Brazilian Jiu Jitsu	12	10
Karate	9	11
Kung Fu	12	15

55. Which activity has the lowest ratio of males to females?
    a. Judo
    b. Brazilian Jiu Jitsu
    c. Karate
    d. Kung Fu

56. For all the students listed, about what percent of the students are involved in Kung Fu?
    a. 15%
    b. 20%
    c. 27%
    d. 29%

57. If 3 more males and 4 more females join Karate, what percent of the students will be in this club?
    a. 15%
    b. 20%
    c. 27%
    d. 29%

The following line graph shows earnings for the three divisions of Steinberg Lumber Company throughout the four quarters in 2009. Use the information presented to answer questions 58 through 60.

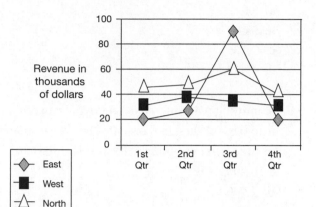

58. Which of the following statements is true?
   a. The East Division consistently brought in more revenue than the other 2 divisions.
   b. The North Division consistently brought in more revenue than the West Division.
   c. The West Division consistently out performed the East Division.
   d. Both **b** and **c** are true.

59. What is the percent decrease in revenue for the North Division when analyzing dollar amounts from the 3rd and 4th quarters?
   a. $33\frac{1}{3}\%$
   b. 40%
   c. 50%
   d. 60%

60. During the year 2009, Steinberg Lumber secured a major contract with a developer in Canada. The East and North Divisions both supplied lumber for this project. Which of the following statements seems to be supported by the data?
   a. The West Division was angry that the other two divisions supplied the lumber for this contract.
   b. The next big contract will be covered by the West Division.
   c. The contract with the Canadian developer was secured in the third quarter.
   d. The contract with the Canadian developer was secured in the fourth quarter.

61. 76,000 milliliters is equivalent to how many liters?
   a. 7.6 liters
   b. 76 liters
   c. 760 liters
   d. 7,600 liters

62. 2,808 inches is equivalent to how many yards?
   a. 234
   b. 110
   c. 78
   d. 36

63. What is the sum of 5 yards 2 feet, 8 yards 1 foot, 3 yards $\frac{1}{2}$ foot, and 4 yards 6 inches?
   a. 20 yards $\frac{1}{2}$ foot
   b. 20 yards 1 foot
   c. 21 yards 1 foot
   d. 21 yards $\frac{1}{2}$ foot

64. There are 12 yards of twine on a roll. Danielle cuts off 2 feet of twine for a project. How many *feet* of twine are left on the roll?
   a. 2
   b. 34
   c. 36
   d. 142

Use the following conversion chart to answer questions 65 and 66.

LIQUID MEASURE
8 oz. = 1 c.
1 pt. = 2 c.
1 qt. = 2 pt.
4 qt. = 1 gal.

65. How many ounces are in 2 pints?
- **a.** 16 ounces
- **b.** 32 ounces
- **c.** 44 ounces
- **d.** 64 ounces

66. 364 ounces is equivalent to how many quarts?
- **a.** 182 quarts
- **b.** 91 quarts
- **c.** 22.75 quarts
- **d.** 11.375 quarts

67. A rectangular tract of land measures 860 feet by 560 feet. Approximately how many acres is this? (1 acre = 43,560 square feet.)
- **a.** 12.8 acres
- **b.** 11.06 acres
- **c.** 10.5 acres
- **d.** 8.06 acres

68. Two lengths of pipe will be fitted together. If one pipe is 6 ft. 7 in. and the other is 9 ft. 11 in., how long will the new pipe be?
- **a.** 15 ft. 6 in.
- **b.** 15 ft. 18 in.
- **c.** 16 ft. 6 in.
- **d.** 17 ft. 16 in.

69. A commercial box of nails weighs 34 lbs. If each nail weighs approximately 1 oz., how many nails are in the box? (1 lb. = 16 oz. The weight of the box is negligible.)
- **a.** 34
- **b.** 544
- **c.** 2,176
- **d.** 4,352

70. A canning plant received 1.5 tons of tuna that is to be packaged in 8 oz. cans. How many cans of tuna will be produced from this shipment?
- **a.** 6,000
- **b.** 7,000
- **c.** 8,000
- **d.** 9,000

71. Marguerite is redoing her bathroom floor. Each imported tile measures $1\frac{2}{7}$ inches by $1\frac{4}{5}$ inches. What is the area of each tile?
- **a.** $1\frac{8}{35}$ square inches
- **b.** $1\frac{11}{135}$ square inches
- **c.** $2\frac{11}{35}$ square inches
- **d.** $3\frac{3}{35}$ square inches

72. A rectangular swimming pool measures 160 feet long and 80 feet wide. What is the perimeter of the pool in yards?
- **a.** 480
- **b.** 160
- **c.** 240
- **d.** 280

73. The standard distance of a marathon is 26.2 miles. If the length of a walker's stride is 1.96 feet, approximately how many steps does she take to walk a marathon?

←—1.96 ft—→

  a. 23,527
  b. 70,580
  c. 138,336
  d. 271,139

74. A contractor has 80 feet of fencing to enclose a Jacuzzi area. There should be a walkway around the Jacuzzi that is 3 feet wide. What shape of Jacuzzi should be built in order to have the largest amount of area with the given perimeter?
  a. A square
  b. A cross
  c. A rectangle
  d. A circle

75. A cube-shaped piece of metal must be coated with a special Teflon covering. If the cube has a side of 15 cm, what is the total surface area that needs to be coated?
  a. 600 cm^2
  b. 900 cm^2
  c. 1,350 cm^2
  d. 3,375 cm^2

76. A cylindrical tank is 10 ft. tall with a diameter of 4 ft. What is the potential volume of the tank?
  a. 40 ft.^{3}
  b. 54.5 ft.^{3}
  c. 62.8 ft.^{3}
  d. 125.6 ft.^{3}

77. How much fabric is required to cover a box if the length is 2.5 ft., the width is 8 in., and the height is 3 in.?
  a. 354 in.^{2}
  b. 452 in.^{2}
  c. 708 in.^{2}
  d. 2,160 in.^{2}

78. If the volume of a cube is 27 cubic centimeters, what is its surface area?
  a. 3 cm^2
  b. 6 cm^2
  c. 9 cm^2
  d. 54 cm^2

79. The length of a rectangle is equal to 3 inches more than twice the width. If the width is 2 in., what is the area of the rectangle?
  a. 7 square inches
  b. 14 square inches
  c. 18 square inches
  d. 21 square inches

80. Hannah's yard is square. A lamp is placed in the center of her yard. The lamp shines a radius of 10 feet on her yard, which is 20 feet on each side. How much of the yard, in square feet, is NOT lit by the lamp?
  a. 400π
  b. 40 – 10π
  c. 400 – 10π
  d. 400 – 100π

Answers

1. b. To find a *difference*, just subtract. The term *positive difference* means you are solving for a positive answer. This means you should subtract the smaller number from the larger number: $10,752 - 675 = 10,077$. (See Chapter 3.)

2. c. To find the product, just multiply: $523 \times 13 = 6,799$. Rounding to the nearest hundred yields 6,800. (See Chapter 3.)

3. b. First, find the two products: $3 \times 2 = 6$ and $4 \times 5 = 20$. Next, add these two products together: $6 + 20 = 26$. (See Chapter 3.)

4. d. To find a difference, you subtract: $582 - 73 = 509$. (See Chapter 3.)

5. b. The rules for the order of operations state that division should be done before addition. Recall **PEMDAS**: *parentheses, exponents, multiplication, division, addition, subtraction.* $7,995 \div 15 = 533$. Next add: $589 + 533 = 1,122$. (See Chapter 3.)

6. d. Consider **PEMDAS**: *parentheses, exponents, multiplication, division, addition, subtraction.* Here you must solve the division first: $540 \div 6 = 90$. The equation becomes $90 + 3 \times 24$. Again, considering PEMDAS, you know you should calculate the multiplication first. $3 \times 24 = 72$, so the equation reduces to $90 + 72 = 162$. (See Chapter 3.)

7. a. When raising a power of a base to another power, you just multiply the exponents. (See Chapter 3.)

8. a. $7^3 = 7 \times 7 \times 7$, which equals $49 \times 7 = 343$. (See Chapter 3.)

9. d. The prime factorization can contain only primes and must multiply to the given number (60). Answer choices **a** and **c** can be eliminated because they contain numbers that are not prime (10, 30, and 6). Answer choice **b** can be eliminated because it multiplies to 80, not 60. Answer choice **d** is correct because all numbers are prime and $2 \times 2 \times 3 \times 5 = 60$. (See Chapter 3.)

10. d. A factor is a number that divides evenly (no remainder) into another number. 13 is the only answer choice that does not divide into 36 evenly. (See Chapter 3.)

11. c. Adding together the whole numbers results in 13. To add the fractions, you need to first find the lowest common denominator of 7 and 5, or 35. The new numerators, 15 and 14, add up to 29, so the fraction part of your answer is $\frac{29}{35}$. (See Chapter 4.)

12. d. The lowest common denominator is 24: $\frac{20}{24} + \frac{9}{24} = \frac{29}{24}$. Convert to a mixed number: $1\frac{5}{24}$. (See Chapter 4.)

13. a. First, find the least common denominator of the fractions, which is 9, then add the fractions: $\frac{6}{9} + \frac{2}{9} = \frac{8}{9}$. Now add the whole numbers: $43 + 20 = 63$. Now add the results of the two equations: $\frac{8}{9} + 63 = 63\frac{8}{9}$. (See Chapter 4.)

14. a. Again, in order to subtract the fractions, you must first find the least common denominator, which in this case is 40. The equation is then $\frac{35}{40} - \frac{24}{40} = \frac{11}{40}$. (See Chapter 4.)

15. d. The lowest common denominator is 21: $\frac{12}{21} - \frac{7}{21} = \frac{5}{21}$. (See Chapter 4.)

16. d. The first step in solving this problem is to subtract to get $-\frac{6}{3}$. This reduces to -2. (See Chapter 4.)

17. a. The product when multiplying reciprocals is always 1. (See Chapter 4.)

18. c. Multiply across: $\frac{10}{216}$. Then reduce to lowest terms to get the answer: $\frac{5}{108}$. (See Chapter 4.)

19. a. Multiply across to get the answer: $\frac{28}{45}$.
(See Chapter 4.)

20. b. The correct answer is $1\frac{1}{6}$. (See Chapter 4.)

21. d. The places to the right of the decimal point are (in order): the *tenths place, hundredths place, thousandths place*, and so on. You are looking for a 3 in the hundredths place, which is the second spot to the right of the decimal point. Only choice **d** has a 3 in this place:

UNITS (ONES)	TENTHS	HUNDREDTHS	THOUSANDTHS	TEN THOUSANDTHS	HUNDRED THOUSANDTHS
0.	0	3	5	1	4

Note that choice **a** has a 6 in the hundreds place and NOT the *hundredths* place. (See Chapter 5.)

22. d. 25.682 has a 6 in the tenths place. Because the number in the hundredths place (the 8) is greater than 5, you will round up to 25.7.

TENS	UNITS (ONES)	TENTHS	HUNDREDTHS	THOUSANDTHS
2	5.	6	8	2

You round up because $8 \geq 5$. (See Chapter 5.)

23. c. $\frac{7}{25}$ can be translated into *hundredths* by multiplying by $\frac{4}{4}$. Thus, $\frac{7}{25} \times \frac{4}{4} = \frac{28}{100}$. 28 *hundredths* can be rewritten as 0.28, choice **c**. (See Chapter 5.)

24. c. *Sum* means "add." Line up the decimal points and add:

$$\begin{array}{r} 2.523 \\ +\ 6.76014 \\ \hline 9.28314 \end{array}$$

(See Chapter 5.)

25. b. 14.02 is equivalent to 14.020. Line up all the decimal points and add:

$$\begin{array}{r} 14.020 \\ .987 \\ +\quad .145 \\ \hline 15.152 \end{array}$$

(See Chapter 5.)

26. b. Line up the decimal points and subtract:

$$\begin{array}{r} 324.0073 \\ -87.663 \\ \hline 236.3443 \end{array}$$

(See Chapter 5.)

27. a. Rewrite 8.3 as its equivalent 8.300. Line up the decimal points and subtract:

$$\begin{array}{r} 8.300 \\ -\ 1.725 \\ \hline 6.575 \end{array}$$

(See Chapter 5.)

28. b. First, multiply in the usual fashion (ignoring the decimal points): $0.88 \times 0.22 = 1,936$. Next, you need to insert the decimal point in the correct position, so take note of the position of each decimal point in the two factors:

0.88	The decimal point is **2 places to the left.**
0.22	The decimal point is **2 places to the left.**
In the answer...	The decimal point should be **2 + 2, or 4 places to the left.**

1,936 becomes 0.1936, choice **b.** (See Chapter 5.)

29. a. First multiply 0.125 by 8 to get 1. Next multiply 1 by 0.32 to get 0.32. This is choice **a.** (See Chapter 5.)

30. b. The division problem $512 \div 0.256$ can be solved with long division. Move the decimal point three places to the right in each number:

$$.256\overline{)512.000}$$

Next, divide as usual to get 2,000, choice **b.** (See Chapter 5.)

31. b. Given a 2:14 ratio, the total = 16. So, $\frac{2}{16}$ of 96 are full-time firefighters, or $\frac{2}{16} \times 96 = 12$. (See Chapter 6.)

32. b. Given a 4:3 ratio, the total = 7. So, $\frac{3}{7}$ of 28 are women, or $\frac{3}{7} \times 28 = 12$. (See Chapter 6.)

33. a. There is a 7:2 ratio of clerical workers to executive workers, so the total is 9. Since there are 81 clerical workers to executive workers *combined*, the total of 9 has been multiplied by 9. This means you can take the 7:2 ratio and use the 7 (the part that represents the clerical workers) and multiply by 9 to get: $7 \times 9 = 63$ clerical workers. (See Chapter 6.)

34. d. Set the two Republican-Democrat ratios as equal: Republicans in the city council/Democrats in the city council = Republicans on the committee/Democrats on the committee. Based on the information you are given, this is $\frac{34}{51} = \frac{4}{\text{Democrats}}$ on the committee. Cross multiply: $34 \times$ Democrats on the committee $= 51 \times 4$. The Democrats on the committee $= 51 \times \frac{4}{34} = \frac{204}{34} = 6$. (See Chapter 6.)

35. d. Convert each choice into cost per ounce by dividing:
 a. $\$1 \div 5$ oz. $= \$0.2$
 b. $\$2 \div 11$ oz. $= \$0.181818\ldots$
 c. $\$4 \div 22$ oz. $= \$0.181818\ldots$
 d. $\$7 \div 40 = \$.175$
Thus, the lowest unit price is $.175, choice **d.** (See Chapter 6.)

36. c. First, put 26.5 over $100 = \frac{26.5}{100}$. This is not an answer choice, so you need to reduce. Multiply $\frac{26.5}{100}$ by $\frac{10}{10}$ before reducing: $\frac{26.5}{100} \times \frac{10}{10} = \frac{265}{1,000}$. Now you reduce $\frac{265}{1,000} = \frac{53}{200}$. (See Chapter 6.)

37. c. To change a percent to a fraction, first put the percent over 100. Thus, $0.37\% = \frac{0.37}{100}$. In order to get a whole number in the numerator, multiply the fraction by $\frac{100}{100}$. Thus, $\frac{0.37}{100} \times \frac{100}{100} = \frac{37}{10,000}$. (See Chapter 6.)

38. d. You need to find 17%, or 0.17 of 6,800. Remember that *of* means multiply: $0.17 \times 6,800 = 1,156$. (See Chapter 6.)

39. c. The question "What percent of $\frac{8}{9}$ is $\frac{2}{3}$?" can be expressed mathematically as $\frac{?}{100} \times \frac{8}{9} = \frac{2}{3}$. Divide both sides by $\frac{8}{9}$ to get $\frac{?}{100} = \frac{2}{3} \div \frac{8}{9}$ or $\frac{?}{100} = \frac{2}{3} \times \frac{9}{8}$. This simplifies to $\frac{?}{100} = \frac{18}{24}$, or $\frac{?}{100} = \frac{3}{4}$. Multiply both sides by 100 to get $? = \frac{300}{4}$, so $? = 75$. (See Chapter 6.)

40. d. Here, the part is greater than the whole, so the answer is going to be greater than 100%. The question "What percent of 9 is 36?" can be expressed mathematically as $\frac{?}{100} \times 9 = 36$. Divide both sides by 9 to get $\frac{?}{100} = 36 \div 9$ or $\frac{?}{100} = 4$. Multiply both sides by 100 to get $? = 4 \times 100 = 400\%$. (See Chapter 6.)

41. c. To find the cost per sweater, divide the total cost ($900) by the number of sweaters (120). $900 divided by 120 = $7.50. (See Chapter 7.)

42. b. With both pipes working, the pool is being filled at a rate of 11 gallons per minute. (5 gallons/minute + 6 gallons/minute = 11 gallons/minute.) Now, divide the total amount of gallons in the pool (6,000) by the rate (11 gallons/minute); 6,000 divided by 11 = 545.45. Round to the nearest minute: 545 minutes. (See Chapter 7.)

43. c. Calculate how much the worker will make for a 10-hour day. At $15.50 per hour, the worker will make $155.00 per day working 10-hour days ($15.50 times 10). (See Chapter 7.)

44. a. The first cleaner costs $2.75 for 44 ounces. Since the cost per ounce is needed, divide $2.75 by 44 to get about $0.0625 per ounce, or about $0.06 per ounce. The second cleaner costs $3.70 for 55 ounces. $3.70 divided by 55 = $0.067 per ounce, or about $0.07 per ounce. Therefore, the first cleaner is the better buy because it is cheaper per ounce. (See Chapter 7.)

45. d. For the highway portion of the trip, Joe will average 65 mph for 13 miles. Since 13 is $\frac{1}{5}$ of 65, this portion of the trip will take Joe $\frac{1}{5}$ of an hour, or 12 minutes. For the remaining 12 miles of the trip Joe will average 24 mph. Since 12 is half of 24, this portion of the trip will take half an hour or 30 minutes. The total time will be 12 minutes + 30 minutes = 42 minutes. To arrive by 1:30 P.M., Joe must leave no later than 12:48 P.M. since 1:30 P.M. − 42 minutes = 12:48 P.M. Therefore, the correct answer is 12:48 P.M. (See Chapter 7.)

46. a. The 1,400 square foot home costs about $14.29 per square foot: $20,000 divided by 1,400 square feet = $14.29 per square foot. The 2,200 square foot home costs about $12.73 per square foot: $28,000 divided by 2,200 square feet = $12.73 per square foot. The 2,500 square foot home costs about $14 per square foot: $35,000 divided by 2,500 square feet = $14 per square foot. The cheapest price per square foot is $12.73 by Smithco. If this company is hired to construct 2,800 square foot homes, it will cost $35,644 per home: 2,800 square feet times $12.73 per square foot = $35,644. Rounded to the nearest thousand, the answer is $36,000. (See Chapter 7.)

47. c. In order to find out how many hours she worked, divide the total amount by the hourly wage ($\frac{90}{15} = 6$); 6 hours. (See Chapter 7.)

48. b. When purchasing multiple items for the same price, use multiplication to find the answer. ($12 \times 7.45 = 89.40$); $89.40. (See Chapter 7.)

49. a. Subtract the total purchase from the amount the customer paid ($20 − 14.52 = 5.48$); $5.48 is the change. (See Chapter 7.)

50. b. The tax for this purchase is calculated by multiplying the pre-tax price by the % tax written in decimal form. ($20 \times 0.0715 = 1.43$). Then, add the tax to the original sales amount for the total ($20 + 1.43 = 21.43$); $21.43 is the total. (See Chapter 7.)

51. d. The fastest swimmer will have the quickest time. 37.89 is the fastest. Thus, Risa is the fastest swimmer. (See Chapter 8.)

52. a. 22% is spent on food. When you combine transportation (9%) and clothing (4%), the sum is 13%. Thus, the amount spent on food is 22% − 13% = 9% greater. (See Chapter 8.)

53. c. Housing consumes 30% of the monthly budget. 30% of $4,000 is calculated by multiplying: $30\% \times \$4,000 = 0.30 \times \$4,000 = \$1,200$. (See Chapter 8.)

54. b. They save 10% of $4,000 each month: $0.10 \times \$4,000 = \$400$. Over the course of a year they will save $400 per month × 12 months = $4,800. (See Chapter 8.)

55. d. The M:F (male to female) ratios are as follows:
Judo: $\frac{11}{13} = 0.85$
Brazilian Jiu Jitsu: $\frac{12}{10} = 1.2$
Karate: $\frac{9}{11} = 0.82$
Kung Fu: $\frac{12}{15} = 0.8$
Here, 0.8 is the least value, so a $\frac{12}{15}$ ratio is the smallest M:F ratio listed. (See Chapter 8.)

56. d. This question is easily solved by adding a column and row labeled "Total" onto the side and bottom of the given chart. Now you can easily see that 27 students out of the 93 total are taking Kung Fu. $\frac{27}{93} = 0.29$. To write these values as a percent, simply move the decimal point two places to the right and add the percent symbol: 29%. (See Chapter 8.)

57. c. Using the new information, now 27 out of 100 students are in Karate. $\frac{27}{100} = 27\%$. (See Chapter 8.)

58. b. Looking at the graph, you see that the line for *North* (the line with triangular points) is always higher than the line for *West* (the line with the square points). All other statements are not supported by the data in the graph. Thus, only choice **b** is true. (See Chapter 8.)

59. a. Here the revenue in thousands of dollars decreases from 60 to 40. Thus, the difference is 20. As compared with the original 60, this represents $\frac{20}{60} = 0.333$. To express this as a percent, just move the decimal point 2 places to the right: $0.3333 \rightarrow 33\frac{1}{3}\%$. (See Chapter 8.)

60. c. Since you are told that this was a "major" contract, the statement best supported by the data is choice **c**: "The contract with the Canadian developer was secured in the third quarter." The data supports this statement because both the East and North Divisions had a significant revenue increase during the third quarter, which might be indicative of having a large contract for that quarter. (See Chapter 8.)

61. b. 1 liter = 1,000 milliliters so you can use the conversion factor $\frac{1\,\text{L}}{1,000\,\text{mL}}$ to convert the milliliters into liters. $76,000\,\text{mL} \times \frac{1\,\text{L}}{1,000\,\text{mL}} = 76\,\text{L}$. (See Chapter 9.)

62. c. Since there are 36 inches per yard, use the conversion factor $\frac{1\,\text{yd.}}{36\,\text{in.}}$ and multiply: $2,808\,\text{in.} \times \frac{1\,\text{yd.}}{36\,\text{in.}} = 78\,\text{yd.}$ (See Chapter 9.)

63. c. First, note that 4 yards 6 inches is the same as 4 yards $\frac{1}{2}$ foot, as this will help you combine units. Next, add up all the values:

$$5\ \text{yd.}\ 2\ \text{ft.}$$
$$8\ \text{yd.}\ 1\ \text{ft.}$$
$$3\ \text{yd.}\ \tfrac{1}{2}\ \text{ft.}$$
$$+\ 4\ \text{yd.}\ \tfrac{1}{2}\ \text{ft.}$$
$$\overline{20\ \text{yd.}\ 4\ \text{ft.}}$$

Next, note that 4 feet = 1 yard + 1 foot. Thus, 20 yards 4 feet can be converted to 21 yards 1 foot. (See Chapter 9.)

64. b. First convert the 12 yards into feet: 12 yd. × $\frac{3 \text{ ft.}}{1 \text{ yd.}}$ = 36 feet at the start. Next, Danielle cuts 2 feet off, so 34 feet are left. (See Chapter 9.)

65. b. Using the chart, you can make conversion factors where you will cross off *pints* and end up with *ounces* (oz.). Thus, you multiply: 2 pints × $\frac{2 \text{ c.}}{1 \text{ pt.}}$ × $\frac{8 \text{ oz.}}{1 \text{ c.}}$ = 32 ounces. (See Chapter 9.)

66. d. Using the chart, you can make conversion factors where you will cross off ounces and end up with *quarts* (qt.): 364 ounces × $\frac{1 \text{ c.}}{8 \text{ oz.}}$ × $\frac{1 \text{ pt.}}{2 \text{ c.}}$ × $\frac{1 \text{ qt.}}{2 \text{ pt.}}$ = $\frac{364}{32}$ = 11.375 quarts. (See Chapter 9.)

67. b. First, calculate the area in square feet. The area of a rectangle is *lw*, so $A = lw$ = 860 feet × 560 feet = 481,600 square feet. Next, use the conversion factor $\frac{1 \text{ acre}}{43,560 \text{ ft.}^2}$ and multiply: 481,600 ft^2 × $\frac{1 \text{ acre}}{43,560 \text{ ft.}^2}$ = 11.056 acres = 11.06 acres. (See Chapter 9.)

68. c. Add the two pipes together and then the inches will need to be simplified (6 ft. 7 in. + 9 ft. 11 in. = 15 ft. 18 in.). It is not proper to leave the 18 in. as it is. 18 in. is the same as 1 ft. 6 in. (there are 12 inches in a foot, so subtract 12 from 18 to find that there are 1 ft. 6 in. in 18 in.). Add 15 ft. + 1 ft. 6 in. to get 16 ft. 6 in. (See Chapter 9.)

69. b. Use the conversion to calculate; if 1 lb. = 16 oz., then multiply 34 by 16 to find the total number of oz. (34 × 16 = 544). If each nail weighs 1 oz., there are 544 nails in a 34 lb. box. (See Chapter 9.)

70. a. 1.5 tons is the same as 3,000 lbs (1.5 × 2,000 = 3,000) and 3,000 lbs. is the same as 48,000 ounces (3,000 × 16 = 48,000). If each can holds 8 oz., then 6,000 cans will be produced ($\frac{48,000}{8}$ = 6,000). (See Chapter 9.)

71. c. Area = *lw*. First, convert the mixed numbers to improper fractions: $1\frac{2}{7}$ inches = $\frac{9}{7}$ inches and $1\frac{4}{5}$ inches = $\frac{9}{5}$ inches. Next, use these fractions in the formula: Area = $lw = \frac{9}{7} \times \frac{9}{5}$ = $\frac{81}{35}$ square inches = $2\frac{11}{35}$ square inches. (See Chapter 10.)

72. b. The perimeter of a rectangle is the sum of all its sides: 160 + 160 + 80 + 80 = 480 feet. Next, convert to yards by multiplying 480 with the conversion factor $\frac{1 \text{ yd.}}{3 \text{ ft.}}$: 480 feet × $\frac{1 \text{ yd.}}{3 \text{ ft.}}$ = 160 yards. (See Chapter 10.)

73. b. Convert 26.2 miles to feet, and divide by the length of the walker's stride to find how many steps she takes in a marathon: 1 mile = 5,280 feet, so 26.2 miles = 138,336 feet. Divide 138,336 by 1.96 feet per step to get 70,579.6. Round to the nearest whole number to get 70,580 steps. (See Chapter 10.)

74. d. A circle will provide the largest area. In order to find the area of the circle, you must find the radius using the circumference (perimeter), which is 12.73 ft. ($C = 3.14 \times 2 \times r$: 80 = 3.14 × 2 × *r*: *r* = 12.73). The area of a circle is calculated by $A = 3.14r^2$ giving a total of 509.8 ft^2. If a square shape were built, the sides would be 20 × 20 ($\frac{80}{4}$ = 20) giving an area of only 400 ft.^{2} (20 × 20 = 400). Playing around with numbers for a rectangle will show that the area would not be able to exceed the circle. (See Chapter 10.)

75. c. The total surface area is 1,350 cm^2. Find the surface area of one side and then multiply by 6 because a cube has six equal faces. The surface area of one side is 225 (15^2 = 15 × 15 = 225) for a total of 1,350 (6 × 225 = 1,350). (See Chapter 10.)

76. d. Volume of a cylinder is calculated by finding the area of the base and multiplying it by the height of the cylinder. The area of the base is a circle and is calculated by $\pi r^2 = A$. The radius is half of the diameter; use 3.14 as an approximation for π ($3.14 \times (2)^2$ = 3.14 × 4 = 12.56). The entire volume is 125.6 ft^3 (12.56 × 10 = 125.6). (See Chapter 10.)

77. c. You are finding the surface area of the box with dimensions of 30 in. $(2.5 \times 12 = 30) \times$ 8 in. $\times$ 3 in. There are six sides to a box— Front/Back, Side/Side, Top/Bottom. The front surface area is 90 $(30 \times 3 = 90)$, the side area is 24 $(8 \times 3 = 24)$, and the top area is 240 $(30 \times 8 = 240)$. The total of the front, side, and top is 354 $(90 + 24 + 240 = 354)$ and all that is left is doubling it to find the rest of the box $(354 \times 2 = 708)$. (See Chapter 10.)

78. d. The volume formula for a cube is $V = s^3$, so here $s^3 = 27$ and $s = 3$ cm. The surface area of one face is $s^2 = 3^2 = 9$ cm^2. Since there are six faces, the total surface area is 6×9 cm$^2 = 54$ cm^2.

79. b. "The length of a rectangle is equal to 4 inches more than twice the width," can be expressed mathematically as $l = 2w + 3$. We know $w = 2$, so $l = (2)(2) + 3 = 7$. The area is then $A = lw = 7 \times 2 = 14$ square inches.

80. d. The area of the dark yard is the area of her square yard $(A = s^2)$ minus the circle of light around the lamp $(A = (\pi r^2)$.

20 ft

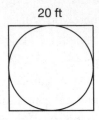

Thus, the dark area $= 20^2 - (\pi \times 10^2)$, or $400 - 100\pi$.

13 ▶ Practice Exam 2

O n this practice exam, you will encounter 80 questions covering the topics you have studied in Chapters 4 through 10. You should have a pencil and scrap paper handy; however, do not use a calculator.

It is not necessary to take this practice exam under timed conditions. If you choose to time yourself, however, allow about 40 minutes to complete this practice exam.

When you are finished, check the answer key on page 170 carefully to assess your results. Good luck!

1.	a	b	c	d	28.	a	b	c	d	55.	a	b	c	d
2.	a	b	c	d	29.	a	b	c	d	56.	a	b	c	d
3.	a	b	c	d	30.	a	b	c	d	57.	a	b	c	d
4.	a	b	c	d	31.	a	b	c	d	58.	a	b	c	d
5.	a	b	c	d	32.	a	b	c	d	59.	a	b	c	d
6.	a	b	c	d	33.	a	b	c	d	60.	a	b	c	d
7.	a	b	c	d	34.	a	b	c	d	61.	a	b	c	d
8.	a	b	c	d	35.	a	b	c	d	62.	a	b	c	d
9.	a	b	c	d	36.	a	b	c	d	63.	a	b	c	d
10.	a	b	c	d	37.	a	b	c	d	64.	a	b	c	d
11.	a	b	c	d	38.	a	b	c	d	65.	a	b	c	d
12.	a	b	c	d	39.	a	b	c	d	66.	a	b	c	d
13.	a	b	c	d	40.	a	b	c	d	67.	a	b	c	d
14.	a	b	c	d	41.	a	b	c	d	68.	a	b	c	d
15.	a	b	c	d	42.	a	b	c	d	69.	a	b	c	d
16.	a	b	c	d	43.	a	b	c	d	70.	a	b	c	d
17.	a	b	c	d	44.	a	b	c	d	71.	a	b	c	d
18.	a	b	c	d	45.	a	b	c	d	72.	a	b	c	d
19.	a	b	c	d	46.	a	b	c	d	73.	a	b	c	d
20.	a	b	c	d	47.	a	b	c	d	74.	a	b	c	d
21.	a	b	c	d	48.	a	b	c	d	75.	a	b	c	d
22.	a	b	c	d	49.	a	b	c	d	76.	a	b	c	d
23.	a	b	c	d	50.	a	b	c	d	77.	a	b	c	d
24.	a	b	c	d	51.	a	b	c	d	78.	a	b	c	d
25.	a	b	c	d	52.	a	b	c	d	79.	a	b	c	d
26.	a	b	c	d	53.	a	b	c	d	80.	a	b	c	d
27.	a	b	c	d	54.	a	b	c	d					

1. What is the product of 52 and 22?
a. 30
b. 74
c. 104
d. 1,144

2. How much greater is the sum of 523 and 65 than the product of 25 and 18?
a. 138
b. 545
c. 588
d. 33,545

3. $78 \times (32 + 12) =$
a. 2,508
b. 3,432
c. 6,852
d. 29,953

4. Which of the following demonstrates the commutative property?
a. $2 + 3 = 4 + 1$
b. $2 + (3 + 4) = (2 + 3) + 4$
c. $2 \times 3 = 3 \times 2$
d. $2 \times (3 \times 4) = (2 \times 3) \times 4$

5. Which of the following demonstrates the associative property?
a. $4 + 5 = 5 + 4$
b. $2 \times (3 + 4) = (2 \times 3) + 4$
c. $4 \times 5 = 5 \times 4$
d. $2 \times (3 \times 4) = (2 \times 3) \times 4$

6. Which of the following demonstrates the distributive property?
a. $(4 \times 5) + 1 = 4 \times (5 + 1)$
b. $4 \times (5 + 1) = 4 \times 5 + 4 \times 1$
c. $4 \times 5 \times 1 = 1 \times 5 \times 4$
d. $(4 + 5) + 1 = 4 + (5 + 1)$

7. 4 is a factor of
a. 1
b. 2
c. 4
d. 14

8. $3 \times 3 \times 3 \times 3 \times 3 \times 3 =$
a. $(3^3)^3$
b. $3^2 \times 3^2 \times 3^2$
c. $3^2 \times 3^3$
d. $(3^4)^2$

9. Which of the following is not a factor of 72?
a. 14
b. 12
c. 9
d. 4

10. 18^3 is how much greater than 16^2?
a. 6,088
b. 5,576
c. 265
d. 68

11. $76\frac{1}{2} + 11\frac{5}{6} =$
a. $87\frac{1}{2}$
b. $88\frac{1}{3}$
c. $88\frac{5}{6}$
d. $89\frac{1}{6}$

12. $4\frac{1}{5} + 1\frac{2}{5} + 3\frac{3}{10} =$
a. $9\frac{1}{10}$
b. $8\frac{9}{10}$
c. $8\frac{4}{5}$
d. $8\frac{6}{15}$

13. $5\frac{1}{3} + 7 + 2\frac{1}{3} =$
a. $14\frac{1}{3}$
b. $\frac{1}{3}$
c. 14
d. $14\frac{2}{3}$

14. $\frac{2}{3} - \frac{1}{5} =$
   a. $\frac{7}{15}$
   b. $\frac{2}{5}$
   c. $\frac{5}{12}$
   d. $\frac{3}{8}$

15. $3\frac{9}{16} - 1\frac{7}{8} =$
   a. $1\frac{11}{16}$
   b. $2\frac{1}{8}$
   c. $2\frac{1}{4}$
   d. $2\frac{5}{16}$

16. $\frac{5}{12} - \frac{3}{8} =$
   a. $\frac{1}{10}$
   b. $\frac{1}{24}$
   c. $\frac{5}{48}$
   d. $\frac{19}{24}$

17. $2\frac{1}{3} \times 1\frac{1}{14} \times 1\frac{4}{5} =$
   a. $1\frac{7}{18}$
   b. $2\frac{1}{2}$
   c. $3\frac{6}{7}$
   d. $4\frac{1}{2}$

18. $7\frac{3}{5} \times \frac{4}{9} =$
   a. $7\frac{4}{15}$
   b. $3\frac{1}{15}$
   c. $7\frac{1}{2}$
   d. $3\frac{17}{45}$

19. $7 \times \frac{2}{5} =$
   a. $\frac{1}{5}$
   b. $17\frac{1}{2}$
   c. $2\frac{4}{5}$
   d. $2\frac{2}{5}$

20. $\frac{1}{6} \div 4\frac{5}{8} =$
   a. $\frac{4}{5}$
   b. $27\frac{3}{4}$
   c. $\frac{37}{48}$
   d. $\frac{4}{111}$

21. 234.816 when rounded to the nearest hundredth is
   a. 200
   b. 234.8
   c. 234.81
   d. 234.82

22. What is 3.133 when rounded to the nearest tenth?
   a. 3
   b. 3.1
   c. 3.2
   d. 3.13

23. Which number sentence is true?
   a. $0.23 \geq 2.3$
   b. $0.023 \leq 0.23$
   c. $0.023 \leq 0.0023$
   d. $0.023 \geq 2.3$

24. $67.104 + 51.406 =$
   a. 11.851
   b. 1,185.1
   c. 118.51
   d. 118.61

25. $\frac{1}{5} + 0.25 + \frac{1}{8} + 0.409 =$
   a. $\frac{1}{13} + 0.659$
   b. $0.659 + \frac{1}{40}$
   c. 0.984
   d. 1.084

26. $12.125 - 3.44 =$
   a. 9.685
   b. 8.785
   c. 8.685
   d. 8.585

27. $89.037 - 27.0002 - 4.02 =$
   a. 62.0368
   b. 59.0168
   c. 58.168
   d. 58.0168

28. $0.15 \times \frac{1}{5} =$
   a. 0.2
   b. 0.3
   c. 0.02
   d. 0.03

29. What is the quotient of $83.4 \div 2.1$ when rounded to the nearest tenth?
   a. 40
   b. 39.71
   c. 39.7
   d. 39.8

30. $375 \div 0.125 =$
   a. 5,625
   b. 3,000
   c. 56.25
   d. 30

31. Two gears are connected together. One complete turn of the handle rotates the first gear exactly five times and the second gear rotates exactly two times. How many rotations of the handle will it take to get the first gear to rotate exactly 11 times?
   a. 6
   b. 3.6
   c. 2.5
   d. 2.2

32. The ratio of 6:3:1 represents the inventory of 6 foot, 8 foot, and 12 foot pieces of wood, respectively. If there are a total of 1,400 pieces of wood, how many 8 foot pieces are there?
   a. 140
   b. 280
   c. 420
   d. 840

33. Ten bagels is what approximate percentage of a dozen bagels?
   a. 16.7%
   b. 76.9%
   c. 81.4%
   d. 83.3%

34. Which number sentence below is false?
   a. $20\% \le \frac{1}{5}$
   b. $25\% = \frac{2}{8}$
   c. $35\% > \frac{24}{50}$
   d. $\frac{3}{4} \le 80\%$

35. Express 12 out of 52 to the nearest percent.
   a. 23%
   b. 24%
   c. 25%
   d. 43%

36. $\frac{4}{5}\%$ is equal to
   a. 80
   b. 8
   c. 0.08
   d. 0.008

37. What percent of the circle is shaded?

   a. 25%
   b. 50%
   c. 75%
   d. 100%

38. What percent of the square is shaded?

    a. 25%

    b. 50%

    c. 75%

    d. 100%

39. Which ratio best expresses the following: five hours is what percent of a day?

    a. $\frac{5}{100} = \frac{x}{24}$

    b. $\frac{5}{24} = \frac{24}{x}$

    c. $\frac{5}{24} = \frac{x}{100}$

    d. $\frac{x}{100} = \frac{24}{5}$

40. If 10% of a number is 45, what would 20% of that number be?

    a. 9

    b. 90

    c. 450

    d. 900

41. 400 books went on sale this week. So far, 120 have been sold. What percent of the books remain?

    a. 15%

    b. 30%

    c. 70%

    d. 80%

42. At an electronics store, all items are sold at 15% above cost. If the store purchased a printer for $85, how much will they sell it for?

    a. $100

    b. $98.50

    c. $97.75

    d. $95.50

43. $8,000 is deposited into a bank account. If interest is compounded semiannually (twice a year) at 5% for 1 year, how much money is in the account at the end of the year? (Use the interest formula: $I = PRT$, where I is the interest, P is the principal amount put into the account, and T is the time.)

    a. $8,175

    b. $8,200

    c. $8,400

    d. $8,405

44. This morning, 160 heads of lettuce were delivered to a local grocer. Due to weather and traveling conditions, 30% of the produce was not suitable for sale. How many heads of lettuce were spoiled?

    a. 40

    b. 42

    c. 48

    d. 56

45. At the start of the day, inventory reports showed that there were 37 drills in stock at the store. After a Father's Day sale, the receipts showed that 9 drills were sold. How many drills were left in stock?

    a. 25

    b. 26

    c. 28

    d. 46

46. The manager of a hardware store is gathering scraps from boards that were originally 12 feet in length. Out of the five pieces of scrap, two were $\frac{1}{4}$ of the original length, 1 was $\frac{1}{3}$ of the original, 1 was $\frac{2}{5}$ the original, and the last one was $\frac{1}{2}$ the original. Find the length, in feet, of all the scraps.

    a. 20.8 feet

    b. 18.7 feet

    c. 17.8 feet

    d. 21 feet

47. A telephone company charges a $0.32 connection fee and 8¢ a minute for calls out of state. How much does it cost to make a 1 hour and 15 minute call out of state?
- **a.** $0.42
- **b.** $4.20
- **c.** $6.00
- **d.** $6.32

48. A contractor received $250 up front to finish a job. He needed to make several purchases to finish the job. The first supplies cost $135.60. However, the contractor returned $12.45 worth of supplies and purchased an additional $69.15 of supplies. How much money is left over?
- **a.** $32.80
- **b.** $45.25
- **c.** $57.70
- **d.** There is no money left over.

49. At a fabric store a customer wants to purchase 5 feet of a particular fabric that sells for $4.50 per yard. How much will it cost for a 5-foot section?
- **a.** $7.50
- **b.** $8.35
- **c.** $21.25
- **d.** $22.50

50. Today, 200 copies of a new book arrived at the local bookstore. Unfortunately, 50 books were damaged. Of those 50 books, 13 could still be sold at a discounted price at an outlet store. What percentage of the damaged stock could still be sold?
- **a.** 26%
- **b.** 6%
- **c.** 25%
- **d.** 75%

Use this chart to answer questions 51 through 53.

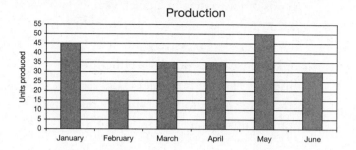

51. A local merchant charted unit production for the first six months of the year. According to the chart, what fraction of the units were produced in April?
- **a.** $\frac{1}{215}$
- **b.** $\frac{215}{35}$
- **c.** $\frac{7}{43}$
- **d.** $\frac{3}{20}$

52. According to the chart, what is the average monthly production, rounded to the nearest tenth of a unit?
- **a.** 32.5 units per month
- **b.** 35.8 units per month
- **c.** 35 units per month
- **d.** 36.2 units per month

53. According to the chart, what was the increase in unit production from February to March?
- **a.** 45.2%
- **b.** 57.1%
- **c.** 75%
- **d.** 80%

54. The chart that follows shows the purchasing trends of customers in a given year. 320 customers exclusively purchase brand A, 120 customers exclusively purchase brand B, and 40 customers purchase either one, differing year to year. What is the greatest percentage of customers typically purchasing brand B during any given month?

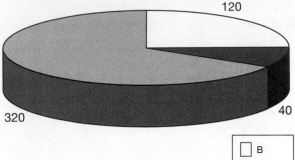

☐	B
■	A or B
▨	A

    a. 25%
    b. up to 33.3%
    c. 68.4%
    d. cannot be determined

Use this table to answer questions 55 and 56.

	DAY SHIFT	EVENING SHIFT	GRAVEYARD SHIFT
# of Employees	154	122	59
Tasks to Complete	385	164	155

The table shows the typical work schedule for a power plant. No employee works more than 1 shift on a given day.

55. How many employees work at the power plant?
    a. 225
    b. 335
    c. 426
    d. 626

56. Which shift has to perform the most tasks per person?
    a. day shift
    b. evening shift
    c. graveyard shift
    d. they are all the same

Use the following chart to answer questions 57 through 60.

The chart shows what two Internet and cable services companies are offering to their customers.

	COMPANY A	COMPANY B
Connection Fee	$12.95	$8.50
Cable	$26.75/month	$27.00/month
High-Speed Internet	$29.99/month	$30.50/month
Combo Package of Cable and High-Speed Internet (no connection fee when this service is selected)	$55.80/month	$54.00/month

57. For a year's subscription, which company offers a better deal for customers who only want cable?
    a. Company A
    b. Company B
    c. They offer the same deal.
    d. not enough information

58. For a year's subscription, which company offers a better deal for customers who only want high-speed Internet?
    a. Company A
    b. Company B
    c. They offer the same deal.
    d. not enough information

59. Which company offers a better deal on premium cable channels?
- **a.** Company A
- **b.** Company B
- **c.** They offer the same deal.
- **d.** not enough information

60. Which company offers the larger discount if a combo package is selected for a year?
- **a.** Company A
- **b.** Company B
- **c.** They provide the same discount.
- **d.** not enough information

61. How many yards are in a mile?
- **a.** 1,760
- **b.** 4,400
- **c.** 5,280
- **d.** 63,360

Use the following chart to answer questions 62 and 63.

ENGLISH/METRIC UNIT APPROXIMATE CONVERSIONS
LENGTH
1 in. = 2.54 cm
1 yard = 0.9 m
1 mi. = 1.6 km

62. Convert 3 feet 5 inches into an approximate number of centimeters.
- **a.** 104.14 centimeters
- **b.** 65.6 centimeters
- **c.** 51.3 centimeters
- **d.** 16.14 centimeters

63. 5,500 yards is equivalent to about how many meters?
- **a.** 13,970 meters
- **b.** 6,111 meters
- **c.** 9,800 meters
- **d.** 4,950 meters

Use the following equivalency chart to answer questions 64 and 65.

LIQUID MEASURE
8 oz. = 1 c.
2 c. = 1 pt.
2 pt. = 1 qt.
4 qt. = 1 gal.

64. How many ounces are in 3 gallons?
- **a.** 384 ounces
- **b.** 192 ounces
- **c.** 96 ounces
- **d.** 48 ounces

65. A 25-gallon tub of fluid will be poured into containers that each hold half of a quart. If all the containers are filled to capacity, how many will be filled?
- **a.** 50
- **b.** 100
- **c.** 200
- **d.** 250

66. How many ounces are in 5 pints?
- **a.** 10 oz.
- **b.** 20 oz.
- **c.** 40 oz.
- **d.** 80 oz.

67. An 18-gallon barrel of liquid will be poured into containers that each hold half of a pint of fluid. If all the containers are filled to capacity, how many will be filled?
- **a.** 36
- **b.** 72
- **c.** 144
- **d.** 288

Use the following chart as a reference for questions 68 and 69.

METRIC UNITS TO CUSTOMARY UNITS CONVERSIONS
1 cm = .39 in.
1 m = 1.1 yd.
1 km = .6 mi.

68. 3.5 ft. is equivalent to approximately how many meters?
   a. 4 m
   b. 3.85 m
   c. 3.18 m
   d. 18 m

69. 5 yd. 2 ft. is equivalent to approximately how many centimeters?
   a. 523 cm
   b. 79.56 cm
   c. 52.3 cm
   d. 6.63 cm

70. Use $F = \frac{9}{5}C + 32$ to convert 113° F into the equivalent Celsius temperature.
   a. 38°
   b. 45°
   c. 54°
   d. 63°

71. If the radius of a cylindrical tank is 7 cm and its volume is 1,540 cm^3, what is the height in cm?
   a. 10 cm
   b. 15.4 cm
   c. 10π cm
   d. 15.4π cm

72. The largest sector of the following circle graph has an angle equal to how many degrees?

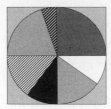

   a. 15 degrees
   b. 45 degrees
   c. 90 degrees
   d. 180 degrees

73. A square with *sides* = 8 in. has the same area of a rectangle with *width* = 4 in. What is the length of the rectangle?
   a. 8 in.
   b. 12 in.
   c. 16 in.
   d. 64 in.

74. A rectangular tract of land measures 440 feet by 1,782 feet. What is the area in acres? (1 acre = 43,560 square feet.)
   a. 14 acres
   b. 16 acres
   c. 18 acres
   d. 20 acres

75. If the area of a circle is 16π square inches, what is the circumference?
   a. 2π inches
   b. 4π inches
   c. 8π inches
   d. 12π inches

76. If the volume of a cube is 8 cubic inches, what is its surface area?
   a. 80 square inches
   b. 40 square inches
   c. 24 square inches
   d. 16 square inches

77. Giorgio is making an "open" box. He starts with a 10×7 rectangle, then cuts 2×2 squares out of each corner. To finish, he folds each side up to make the box. What is the box's volume?

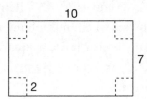

    a. 36 cubic units
    b. 42 cubic units
    c. 70 cubic units
    d. 72 cubic units

78. A cylindrical can measures 4.2 inches in height. Its circular bases of $\frac{1}{2}$ inch radii are removed, and the cylinder flattened out. What is the surface area of the flattened-out cylinder? (Use 3.14 for π.)
    a. 3.297 square inches
    b. 8.54 square inches
    c. 12.1 square inches
    d. 13.188 square inches

79. A point on the outer edge of a wheel is 2.5 feet from the axis of rotation. If the wheel spins at a full rate of 2,640 revolutions per minute, how many miles will the point on the outer edge of the wheel travel in one hour?
    a. 75π
    b. 100π
    c. 112π
    d. 150π

80. What is the perimeter of the shaded area if the shape is a quarter-circle with a radius of 3.5? (Use $\pi = \frac{22}{7}$.)

    a. 7 units
    b. 12.5 units
    c. 22 units
    d. 29 units

Answers

1. d. The product is obtained by multiplying: $52 \times 22 = 1{,}144$. (See Chapter 4.)

2. a. First, calculate the two equations:
The sum of 523 and 65: $523 + 65 = 588$
The product of 25 and 18: $25 \times 18 = 450$
Next, find the difference: $588 - 450 = 138$.
(See Chapter 4.)

3. b. Remember **PEMDAS**: *parentheses, exponents, multiplication, division, addition, subtraction.* Here you must solve the part inside the parentheses first: $32 + 12 = 44$. The equation becomes 78×44. Multiplying, you get 3,432. (See Chapter 4.)

4. c. Note that this question is not looking for a true equation. It is asking which equation represents the commutative property. The commutative property applies for addition and multiplication and can be represented as $a + b = b + a$ or $a \times b = b \times a$. Choice **c** shows this relationship: $2 \times 3 = 3 \times 2$. In other words, the order in which you multiply two numbers does not matter. (See Chapter 4.)

5. d. The associative property applies to grouping of addition or multiplication problems. It can be represented as $a + (b + c) = (a + b) + c$, or $a \times (b \times c) = (a \times b) \times c$. Note that you CANNOT combine addition and multiplication as in choice **b**. $2 \times (3 + 4) \neq (2 \times 3) + 4$. Only choice **d** correctly shows this property: $2 \times (3 \times 4) = (2 \times 3) \times 4$. (See Chapter 4.)

6. b. The distributive property applies to multiplication over addition such as in choice **b**: $4 \times (5 + 1) = 4 \times 5 + 4 \times 1$. Notice that multiplying the sum of the two terms by 4 is equivalent to multiplying each term by 4 and then adding these values. (See Chapter 4.)

7. c. 4 is a factor of 4, plus an infinite number of other numbers. (See Chapter 4.)

8. b. $3 \times 3 \times 3 \times 3 \times 3 \times 3$ is equivalent to 3^6. Choice **b** is equivalent to 3^6 because $3^2 \times 3^2 \times 3^2$ equals 3^{2+2+2}. Remember to add the powers when multiplying numbers with the same base. Choice **a** equals 3^9, choice **c** equals 3^5, and choice **d** equals 3^8. (See Chapter 4.)

9. a. The factors of 72 are 1, 2, 3, 4, 6, 8, 9, 12. 72 also has other factors greater than 12. (See Chapter 4.)

10. b. First, calculate both quantities: $18^3 = 18 \times 18 \times 18 = 5{,}832$ and $16^2 = 16 \times 16 = 256$. Next, in order to find out how much greater the first quantity is, you find the *difference* (by subtracting): $5{,}832 - 256 = 5{,}576$. (See Chapter 4.)

11. b. To work the problem you must first convert $\frac{1}{2}$ to $\frac{3}{6}$, then add. The correct answer is $88\frac{1}{3}$. (See Chapter 5.)

12. b. Convert to the lowest common denominator, which is 10, then add. The correct answer is $8\frac{9}{10}$. (Incorrect answers may result from adding both the numerator and the denominator and from failing to convert fifths to tenths properly.) (See Chapter 5.)

13. d. To add mixed numbers, make sure the fractions have a common denominator. Then, add the numerators and keep the denominator: $\frac{1}{3} + \frac{1}{3} = \frac{2}{3}$. Then add the whole numbers: $5 + 7 + 2 = 14$. Combine these results to reach a final solution of $14\frac{2}{3}$. (See Chapter 5.)

14. a. This is a subtraction of fractions problem. The first step is to find the common denominator, which for 3 and 5 is 15. So, the problem becomes $\frac{10}{15} - \frac{3}{15}$. Now, subtract the numerators: $10 - 3 = 7$. The answer is $\frac{7}{15}$. (See Chapter 5.)

15. a. First, convert the mixed numbers to fractions. Since any number multiplied by 1 retains its identity, we have: $3\frac{9}{16} = (3)(\frac{16}{16}) + \frac{9}{16} = \frac{48}{16} + \frac{9}{16} = \frac{57}{16}$ and $1\frac{7}{8} = (1)(\frac{8}{8}) + \frac{7}{8} = \frac{8}{8} + \frac{7}{8} = \frac{15}{8}$. Next, find the least common denominator of the two numbers, in this case 16, and convert: $(\frac{15}{8})(\frac{2}{2}) = \frac{30}{16}$. Finally, perform the indicated operation: $\frac{57}{16} - \frac{30}{16} = \frac{27}{16}$ which is equivalent to $(1)(\frac{16}{16}) + \frac{11}{16} = 1\frac{11}{16}$. (See Chapter 5.)

16. b. Before subtracting, you must convert both fractions to twenty-fourths: $\frac{10}{24} - \frac{9}{24} = \frac{1}{24}$. (See Chapter 5.)

17. d. Properly converting the mixed numbers into improper fractions is the first step in finding the answer. Thus $\frac{7}{3} \times \frac{15}{14} \times \frac{9}{5} = \frac{945}{210} = 4\frac{1}{2}$. (See Chapter 5.)

18. d. Convert the mixed number to an improper fraction and multiply: $\frac{38}{5} \times \frac{4}{9} = \frac{152}{45}$. Convert back to a mixed number: $3\frac{17}{45}$. (See Chapter 5.)

19. c. The product of the multiplication is $\frac{14}{5}$, which is $2\frac{4}{5}$ as a mixed number. (See Chapter 5.)

20. d. Convert the mixed number to a fraction. Then invert it because it is the divisor. Multiply: $\frac{1}{6} \times \frac{8}{37} = \frac{8}{222}$. Reduce the fraction to lowest terms: $\frac{4}{111}$. (See Chapter 5.)

21. d. When rounding to the nearest hundredth, you need to truncate (cut short) the number, leaving the last digit in the hundredths place. If the number after the hundredths place is a 5 or higher, you would round up.

HUNDREDS	TENS	UNITS (ONES)	TENTHS	HUNDREDTHS	THOUSANDTHS
2	3	4	8	1	6

↑

6 is higher than 5, so you round the 1 in the hundredths place up to 2. Thus, the answer is 234.82, choice **d**. (See Chapter 6.)

22. b. In order to round to the nearest tenth, you need to cut the number short, leaving the last digit in the tenths place. Here you cut the number short without rounding up because the number in the hundredths place is not ≥ 5.

UNITS (ONES)	TENTHS	HUNDREDTHS	THOUSANDTHS
3	1	3	3

↑

You don't round up because 3 is less than 5. Thus, the answer is 3.1, choice **b**. (See Chapter 6.)

23. b. 0.023 equals $\frac{23}{1,000}$ which is less than 0.23. Thus $0.023 \leq 0.23$. The symbol $\leq$ means *less than or equal to*. (See Chapter 6.)

24. c. Line up the decimal points and add:

$$\begin{array}{r} 67.104 \\ +\ 51.406 \\ \hline 118.51 \end{array}$$

(See Chapter 6.)

25. c. First convert the fractions to decimals: $\frac{1}{5} = 0.2$ and $\frac{1}{8} = 0.125$. Next, line up all the numbers by their decimal points and add (note that zeros are added as place holders):

$$\begin{array}{r} 0.200 \\ 0.250 \\ 0.125 \\ +\ 0.409 \\ \hline 0.984 \end{array}$$

(See Chapter 6.)

26. c. Line up the decimal points (rewriting 3.44 as 3.440) and subtract:

$$\begin{array}{r} 12.125 \\ -\ 3.440 \\ \hline 8.685 \end{array}$$

(See Chapter 6.)

27. d. First rewrite 89.037 as its equivalent 89.0370. Next, subtract 27.0002:

$$\begin{array}{r} 89.0370 \\ -\ 27.0002 \\ \hline 62.0368 \end{array}$$

Now you must subtract 4.02 from the 62.0386. (If you chose choice **a**, you forgot the next step.)

$$\begin{array}{r} 62.0368 \\ -\ 4.02 \\ \hline 58.0168 \end{array}$$

(See Chapter 6.)

28. d. First convert $\frac{1}{5}$ to a decimal: $\frac{1}{5} = 1 \div 5 = 0.2$. Next multiply: $0.15 \times 0.2 = 0.03$. (See Chapter 6.)

29. c. The division problem $83.4 \div 2.1$ can be solved with long division, moving the decimal point in each number one place to the right:

$$2.1\overline{)83.4}$$

Next, divide as usual to get 39.714286. Finally, round to the nearest tenth: 39.7, choice **c**. (See Chapter 6.)

30. b. The division problem $375 \div 0.125$ can be solved with long division, moving the decimal point in each number three places to the right:

$$.125\overline{)375.000}$$

Dividing yields 3,000, choice **b**. (See Chapter 6.)

31. d. There is a ratio of handle to gear of 1:5. The gear needs to turn 11 times, so divide the total number of rotations by the number each handle turn makes ($\frac{11}{5} = 2.2$) to find out how many rotations are needed. (See Chapter 7.)

32. c. The total number of pieces there are can be represented by $6x + 3x + x = 1,400$ because of the ratio that is held. $6x$ represents the number of 6-foot pieces, $3x$ represents the number of 8-foot pieces, and x represents the number of 12-foot pieces. Combine like terms to get $10x = 1,400$, so $x = 140$. Therefore, there are $3(140) = 420$ 8-foot pieces. (See Chapter 7.)

33. d. There are 12 bagels in a dozen bagels, therefore 10 out of 12 bagels is .833 ($\frac{10}{12} = 0.833$). To convert into a percentage, multiply by 100 ($0.833 \times 100 =$ about 83.3%). (See Chapter 7.)

34. c. $20\% = \frac{20}{100}$, or $\frac{1}{5}$, so choice **a** represents a true statement. $25\% = \frac{25}{100} = \frac{1}{4}$, and $\frac{2}{8} = \frac{1}{4}$, so choice **b** is also true. In choice **c**, $35\% = \frac{35}{100}$ and $\frac{24}{50} = \frac{48}{100}$. Thus, the statement $35\% > \frac{24}{50}$ is not true. Choice **c** is therefore the correct answer. In choice **d**, $\frac{3}{4} = 75\%$, which is in fact less than 80%. (See Chapter 7.)

35. a. "12 out of 52" is written as $\frac{12}{52}$. Set up a proportion to see how many hundredths $\frac{12}{52}$ is equivalent to: $\frac{12}{52} = \frac{?}{100}$. Cross multiplying yields $100 \times 12 = 52 \times ?$, or $1,200 = 52 \times ?$. Dividing both sides by 52 yields $? = 23.07623$. When expressed to the nearest percent, this rounds to 23%. (See Chapter 7.)

36. d. It is easier to change $\frac{4}{5}$ into 0.8 before dealing with the percent symbol. $\frac{4}{5}\% = 0.8\% = 0.008$. (See Chapter 7.)

37. b. $\frac{1}{2}$ of the circle is shaded. $\frac{1}{2} = \frac{50}{100} = 50\%$. (See Chapter 7.)

38. c. $\frac{3}{4}$ of the square is shaded. $\frac{3}{4} = \frac{75}{100} = 75\%$. (See Chapter 7.)

39. c. The problem can be restated as: 5 hours is to 24 hours as $x\%$ is to 100%. This is the same as $\frac{5}{24} = \frac{x}{100}$. (See Chapter 7.)

40. b. First figure out what the number is. If 10% of a number is 45, you can call the number "?" and write $0.10 \times ? = 45$. Divide both sides by 0.10 to get $? = 450$. Next, take 20% of 450: $0.20 \times 450 = 90$. (See Chapter 7.)

41. c. 120 out of a total of 400 were sold. Simply set up a proportion to see what this would be equivalent to when expressed out of 100.
$\frac{120}{400} = \frac{?}{100}$
Cross multiplying, you get $120 \times 100 = 400 \times ?$, which is the same as $12,000 = 400 \times ?$, and dividing both sides by 400 yields $? = 30$. Thus 30% were sold, so 70% remain. (See Chapter 8.)

42. c. The printer will sell for 115% of the cost. $115\% \times \$85 = 1.15 \times 85 = 97.75$. This question can also be solved in two steps: 15% of 85 = $12.75 markup. Add $12.75 to $85 (the cost) to get $97.75. (See Chapter 8.)

43. d. Because the interest is compounded semiannually (twice a year), after one-half a year the amount of interest earned $I = PRT = 8,000 \times 0.05 \times \frac{1}{2} = \$200$. Now the account has $8,200 in it. Next, calculate the interest for the second half of the year with $I = PRT = 8,200 \times 0.05 \times \frac{1}{2} = 205$. Thus, the answer is $8,405. (See Chapter 8.)

44. c. The decimal 0.30 represents 30%. Multiply the percent damaged by the number of lettuce heads delivered, $0.30 \times 160 = 48$; 48 heads of lettuce were spoiled. (See Chapter 8.)

45. c. Take the original amount and subtract the sold items ($37 - 9 = 28$); 28 drills are left. (See Chapter 8.)

46. a. In order to find the total amount, you must add up the length of all the pieces ($\frac{1}{4} + \frac{1}{4} + \frac{1}{3} + \frac{2}{5} + \frac{1}{2}$). The first 2 pieces are $\frac{1}{4}$ of 12 feet, or 3 feet and 3 feet. The next piece is $\frac{1}{3}$ of 12 feet, or 4 feet. The fourth piece is $\frac{2}{5}$ of 12 feet, or 4.8 feet. The final piece is $\frac{1}{2}$ of 12 feet, or 6 feet. Now you must add the lengths together to find the total length. Therefore, $3 + 3 + 4 + 4.8 + 6 = 20.8$ feet. (See Chapter 8.)

47. d. Start by converting hours to minutes. Thus, 1 hour and 15 minutes is equivalent to 75 minutes (1 hour = 60 minutes + 15 minutes = 75 minutes) and 75 minutes with $0.08/minute costs $6.00 ($75 \times 0.08 = 6$). The last step is to add on the connection fee of $0.32 for a total of $6.32. (See Chapter 8.)

48. c. Take the original amount and subtract the expenses ($250 - 135.60 - 69.15 = 45.25$) and then add the returned amount because it was refunded ($45.25 + 12.45 = 57.70$) to find the total left, $57.70. (See Chapter 8.)

49. a. The material is sold at a cost per yard but the purchase is in feet. Convert feet into yards by dividing by 3 (3 feet in 1 yard) and then multiply by the cost per yard ($\frac{5}{3} = 1.67$, $1.67 \times 4.50 = 7.5$); $7.50 is the cost for 5 feet of material. (See Chapter 8.)

50. a. 50 of the 200 books were damaged. However, 13 of the 50 damaged books could still be sold. ($\frac{13}{50} = 0.26$ or 26%.) Be careful not to use the original number of 200 to calculate the percentage. (See Chapter 8.)

51. c. First you must find the total production for the 6 months. (45 + 20 + 35 + 35 + 50 + 30 = 215). April produced 35 units, which can be made into a fraction by placing 35 over the total units (215). This fraction can be reduced by dividing the top and bottom by the lowest common factor, which in this case is 5. ($\frac{35}{215} = \frac{7}{43}$); $\frac{7}{43}$ is the total production. (See Chapter 9.)

52. b. To find the average, add up the total and divide by the number of months: $\frac{215}{6} =$ 35.8333 . . . , which rounds to 35.8 per month. (See Chapter 9.)

53. c. February's production was 20 and March's production was 35. The difference in production was 15 (35 − 20 = 15) and 15 of the original 20 is represented by 75% ($\frac{15}{20}$); 75%. (See Chapter 9.)

54. b. If the purchases are spread out pretty evenly throughout the year then it is possible for up to about 33.3% of the sales to be for Product B. There are a total of 480 customers (120 + 40 + 320) and at most for the year there are 160 customers for Product B (120 + 40 = 160). This is represented by about 33.3% ($\frac{160}{480} = 0.333$ . . .). (See Chapter 9.)

55. b. To find the total number of employees, add up the total number in the row with the number of employees (154 + 122 + 59 = 335). (See Chapter 9.)

56. c. To find the tasks per person, divide the tasks by the employees. The day shift has 2.5 tasks per person ($\frac{385}{154} = 2.5$), the night shift has 1.34 ($\frac{164}{122} = 1.34$), and the graveyard shift has 2.63 ($\frac{155}{59} = 2.63$). The graveyard shift has a higher number, so more tasks are performed per person. (See Chapter 9.)

57. b. Cable costs for Company A for a year include the connection fee and 12 months of cable for a total of $333.95 (12.95 + 12(26.75) = 12.95 + 321 = $333.95). Company B costs 332.50 (8.50 + 12(27) = 8.50 + 324 = $332.50) and offers the better deal. (See Chapter 9.)

58. a. Internet costs for Company A for a year include the connection fee and 12 months of service for a total of $372.83 (12.95 + 12(29.99) = 12.95 + 359.88 = $372.83). Company B costs $374.50 (8.50 + 12(30.50) = 8.50 + 366 = 374.50). Company A offers a better deal by a few dollars. (See Chapter 9.)

59. d. There is no information about premium cable channels so there is no way to compare what the companies offer. (See Chapter 9.)

60. b. Without a discount, it would cost $693.83 using Company A for an entire year (12.95 + 12(26.75) + 12(29.99) = 12.95 + 321 + 359.88 = 693.83). With a discount it would only cost $669.60 (12 × 55.80 = 669.60), for a savings of $24.23 (693.83 − 669.60 = 24.23). Without a discount, it would cost $698.50 using Company B for an entire year (8.50 + 12(27) + 12(30.50) = 8.50 + 324 + 366 = 698.50). With a discount it would only cost $648 (12 × 54 = 648), for a savings of $50.50 (698.50 − 648 = 50.50). Company B offers a larger discount from its normal prices compared to its discount/package offer. (See Chapter 9.)

61. a. 1 mile equals 5,280 feet (memorize this). Since there are 3 feet per yard, use the conversion factor $\frac{1\text{ yd.}}{3\text{ ft.}}$ and multiply: 5,280 feet $\times \frac{1\text{ yd.}}{3\text{ ft.}} = 1,760$ yards. (See Chapter 10.)

62. a. First, convert 3 feet 5 inches into 36 inches + 5 inches = 41 inches. Next, use the information given in the chart to make a conversion factor. Since 1 inch = about 2.54 centimeters, and you want to end up with centimeters, you make a conversion factor with inches in the denominator: $\frac{2.54\text{ cm}}{1\text{ in.}}$. Next, multiply: 41 inches $\times \frac{2.54\text{ cm}}{1\text{ in.}} =$ about 104.14 centimeters. (See Chapter 10.)

63. d. The chart says that 1 yard = about 0.9 meters, so you can write the conversion factor as $\frac{0.9\text{ m}}{1\text{ yd.}}$ and multiply: 5,500 yd. $\times \frac{0.9\text{ m}}{1\text{ yd.}}$ = about 4,950 meters. (See Chapter 10.)

64. a. Using the chart you can make conversion factors where you will cross off gallons and end up with *ounces* (oz.): 3 gallons $\times \frac{4\text{ qt.}}{1\text{ gal.}} \times \frac{2\text{ pt.}}{1\text{ qt.}} \times \frac{2\text{ c.}}{1\text{ pt.}} \times \frac{8\text{ oz.}}{1\text{ c.}} = 384$ ounces. (See Chapter 10.)

65. c. First, convert the gallons into quarts: 25 gallons $\times \frac{4\text{ qt.}}{1\text{ gal.}} = 100$ qt. If the fluid will fill 100 one-quart containers, it will then fill 200 $\frac{1}{2}$-quart containers. (See Chapter 10.)

66. d. Using the knowledge that 1 pt. = 2 c. and 1 c. = 8 oz., you can use a series of conversion factors to eliminate pints and keep ounces. Thus, you multiply: 5 pt. $\times \frac{2\text{ c.}}{1\text{ pt.}} \times \frac{8\text{ oz.}}{1\text{ c.}} = 80$ oz.

67. d. Using the knowledge that 1 gal. = 4 qt. and 1 qt. = 2 pt., you can generate a series of conversion factors and multiply them so that you can cross out the units you do not want (gal.) and keep the units you do want: 18 gal $\times \frac{4\text{ qt.}}{1\text{ gal.}} \times \frac{2\text{ pt.}}{1\text{ qt.}} = 144$ pints. Next, remember you are looking for half-pints. 144 pints will fill 288 half-pint containers.

68. c. You should know that 3 ft. = 1 yd. and the chart tells you that 1 m = 1.1 yd. Thus, you can create conversion factors that let you cross off *feet* and end up with *meters*: 3.5 ft. $\times \frac{1\text{ yd.}}{3\text{ ft.}} \times \frac{1\text{ m}}{1.1\text{ yd.}} = 3.18$ m.

69. a. 5 yd. = 15 feet, so 5 yd. 2 ft. = 17 ft. Next, using the fact that 1 ft. = 12 in. and 1 cm = .39 in., you can create conversion factors that let you cross off *feet* and end up with *cm*: 17 ft. $\times \frac{12\text{ in.}}{1\text{ ft.}} \times \frac{1\text{ cm}}{.39\text{ in.}} = 523$ cm.

70. b. Substitute 113 for F in the given equation. Thus, $(F = \frac{9}{5}C + 32)$ becomes $113 = \frac{9}{5}C + 32$; $113 - 32 = \frac{9}{5}C$; $81 = \frac{9}{5}C$; $81 \times \frac{5}{9} = C$; $9 \times 5 = C$; $C = 45$ degrees.

71. a. If you use $\pi = \frac{22}{7}$, and the formula $V = \pi r^2 h$, you get $1,540 = \frac{22}{7} \times 7^2 \times h$. This simplifies to $1,540 = 154 \times h$. Dividing both sides by 154 yields $h = 10$ cm.

72. c. The largest sector takes up a quarter of the circle graph (the gray sector). The interior angles of a circle add to 360 degrees and $\frac{1}{4}$ of $360 = \frac{1}{4} \times 360 = 90$ degrees.

73. c. The area of the square is $A = side^2 = s^2 = 8^2 = 64$ in.^{2}. The area of the rectangle must then also be 64 in.^{2}. Substituting this area and the given width $w = 4$ into the area formula, you get: $A = lw$; $36 = l \times 4$; $l = 64 \div 4 = 16$ in.

74. c. First, calculate the area in square feet: *Area* $= lw = 440$ ft. $\times 1,782$ ft. $= 784,080$ ft.^{2}. Next convert to acres by using the conversion factor $\frac{1\text{ acre}}{43,560\text{ ft.}^2}$ and multiply: $784,080$ ft.$^2 \times \frac{1\text{ acre}}{43,560\text{ ft.}^2} = 18$ acres.

75. c. You are told that *Area* $= 16\pi$. Since $A = \pi r^2$, $16 = r^2$, and $r = 4$. Use this r in the circumference formula: Circumference = $C = 2\pi r = 2\pi \times 4 = 8\pi$ inches.

76. c. The volume formula for a cube is $V = s^3$, so here $s^3 = 8$ and $s = 2$ in. The surface area of one face is $s^2 = 2^2 = 4$ square inches. Since there are six equal faces, the total surface area is 6×4 square inches = 24 square inches. (See Chapter 10.)

77. a. When the 2×2 squares are cut out, the length of the box is 3, and the width is 6. The height is 2:

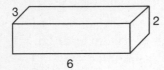

The volume is $3 \times 6 \times 2$, or 36 cubic units. (See Chapter 10.)

78. d. After removing the circular bases, you are left with a flat rectangle. Since the height was 4.2 inches, the length of the rectangle is 4.2 inches. Since the circumference of the bases was $C = 2\pi r = 2 \times 3.14 \times \frac{1}{2} = 3.14$ inches, the width of the rectangle is 3.14 inches. Thus, the area of the new rectangular figure is $lw = 4.2 \times 3.14 = 13.188$ square inches. (See Chapter 10.)

79. d. The point lies on the circumference of a circle with a radius of 2.5 feet. Therefore, the distance that the point travels in one rotation is the length of the circumference of the circle, or $2\pi r = 2\pi(2.5) = 5\pi$ feet. Since the wheel spins at 2,640 revolutions per minute, the point travels $2,640 \times 5\pi$ feet per minute $= 13,200\pi$ feet per minute. Multiplying by 60 to find the distance traveled in one hour, you get $60 \times 13,200\pi = 792,000\pi$ feet per hour. Dividing by 5,280 feet to convert to miles, you get 150π miles per hour. (See Chapter 10.)

80. b. The curved length of the perimeter is one quarter of the circumference of a full circle: $\frac{1}{4}(2\pi r), = \frac{1}{4}(2)(\frac{22}{7})(3.5) = \frac{1}{4}(7 \times \frac{22}{7}) = \frac{1}{4}(22) = 5.5$. The linear (straight) lengths are radii, so the solution is simply $5.5 + 2(3.5)$ or 12.5. (See Chapter 10.)

Glossary of Math Terms

acute angle   An angle that measures between 0 and 90 degrees.

addend   Any number to be added.

addition   An arithmetic operation, in which two or more numbers are combined to get a sum.

altitude   In a triangle, a line that comes from one vertex to the opposite side and forms a right angle.

angle   A shape formed when two rays diverge from one vertex.

area   A measure of how many square units it takes to cover a closed figure.

Associative Law of Addition   The property of numbers that allows you to regroup numbers when adding: $a + (b + c) = (a + b) + c = (a + c) + b$.

Associative property   This property states that parentheses can be moved to group numbers differently when adding or multiplying without affecting the answer.

axis   A reference line drawn on a graph.

backward phrase   A group of words and numbers that describe an operation in which the numbers are given in the opposite order that they will appear in a number sentence.

bar graph   Graphic organizer that uses bars that are differently shaded or colored, that allow for a side-by-side comparison of similar statistics.

base   A number used as a repeated factor in an exponential expression.

chord   A line segment that goes through a circle, with its endpoints on the circle.

circle   The set of all points equidistant from one given point, called the *center*. The center point defines the circle, but it is not on the circle.

circumference   The distance around a circle.

coefficient   The number placed next to a variable in a term.

common denominator   A common multiple of the denominators of two or more fractions.

common factors   A number that divides two or more numbers exactly.

common multiple   A multiple of two or more numbers.

Commutative Property of Addition   The property of numbers that states that order does not matter when adding: $a + b = b + a$.

complementary angles   Two angles that add up to 90 degrees.

cross multiply   To rewrite an equation $\frac{a}{b} = \frac{c}{d}$, in the form $ad = bc$.

cross product   A product of the numerator of one fraction and the denominator of a second fraction.

cubic units   Units of volume formed by multiplying a unit of length by itself twice.

cylinder   A solid with two circular or elliptical flat ends.

decimal system   Numbers related to or based on the number ten. The place value system is a decimal system because the place values (units, tens, hundreds, etc.) are based on ten.

denominator   The bottom number in a fraction. *Example:* 2 is the denominator in $\frac{1}{2}$.

diameter   A line segment that passes through the center of a circle whose endpoints are on the circle.

difference   The difference between two numbers means subtract one number from the other.

directly proportional   A constant relationship between two values, in which a change in one value would also change the other value.

distributive property   When multiplying a sum or a difference by a third number, you can multiply each of the first two numbers by the third number and then add or subtract the products.

dividend   A number that is divided by another number.

divisible by   A number is divisible by a second number if that second number divides *evenly* into the original number. *Example:* 10 is divisible by 5 (10 ÷ 5 = 2, with no remainder). However, 10 is not divisible by 3.

division   An arithmetic operation that shows how many equal quantities add up to a specific number.

divisor   A number that is divided into another number.

equation   A mathematical statement that can use numbers, variables, or a combination of the two and an equal sign.

equilateral triangle   A triangle in which all sides are equal, and all angles are 60 degrees.

even integer   Integers that are divisible by 2, such as −4, −2, 0, 2, 4, and so on.

exponent   A number that tells you how many times a number, the base, is a factor in the product.

factor   A number that can be divided into a larger number without a remainder.

fraction   The result of dividing two numbers. When you divide 3 by 5, you get $\frac{3}{5}$, which equals 0.6. A fraction is a way of expressing a number that involves dividing a top number (the numerator) by a bottom number (the denominator).

graph   A diagram that exhibits a relationship between two sets of numbers.

greatest common factor   The largest of all the common factors of two or more numbers.

histogram   A bar graph that shows how frequently data occur within certain ranges or intervals.

hypotenuse   The longest side of a right triangle.

improper fraction   A fraction whose numerator is greater than or equal to its denominator.

inequality   A sentence that compares quantities that are the greater than, less than, greater than or equal to, or less than or equal to symbols.

integer   A number along the number line, such as −3, −2, −1, 0, 1, 2, 3, and so on. Integers include whole numbers and their negatives.

inversely proportional   A relationship between two values, in which an increase in one causes a decrease in the other.

isosceles triangle A triangle in which two sides are equal in length.

least common denominator The smallest number divisible by two or more denominators.

least common multiple The smallest of all the common multiples of two or more numbers.

leg Side of a right triangle that is not the hypotenuse.

lengths The vertical distance between two ends of an object.

line graph Graphic organizer that uses lines to display information that continues.

metric system An internationally recognized system of measurements based on the meter and kilograms.

minuend The number being subtracted *from*

mixed number A number with an integer part and a fractional part. Mixed numbers can be converted into improper fractions.

multiple of A number is a multiple of a second number if that second number can be multiplied by an integer to get the original number. *Example:* 10 is a multiple of 5 ($10 = 5 \times 2$); however, 10 is not a multiple of 3.

multiplication An arithmetic operation that indicates how many times a number is added to itself.

negative number A number that is less than zero, such as $-1, -18.6, -14$.

number sentences Any mathematical equation that includes numbers, operation, and/or inequality symbols.

numerator The top part of a fraction. *Example:* 1 is the numerator in $\frac{1}{2}$.

obtuse angle An angle that measures more than 90 degrees, but less than 180 degrees.

odd integer An integer that isn't divisible by 2, such as $-5, -3, -1, 1, 3$, and so on.

operand A quantity on which an operation is performed.

order of operations The order in which operations are performed.

parallelogram A quadrilateral with both pairs of opposite sides parallel and equal in length.

PEMDAS Acronym for the order of operations: Parentheses, Exponents, Multiplication, Division, Addition, Subtraction.

percent A ratio that compares numerical data to the hundred. The symbol for percent is %.

perimeter The measure around a figure.

pictograph Graphic organizer that uses pictures to represent a quantity.

pie chart A circle graph that represents a whole, or 100%.

polygon A closed figure with three or more sides.

positive number A number that is greater than zero, such as $2, 42, \frac{1}{2}, 4.63$.

power An exponent to which a given quantity is raised.

prime factorization The process of breaking down factors into prime numbers.

prime number An integer that is divisible only by 1 and itself, such as 2, 3, 5, 7, 11, and so on. All prime numbers are odd, except for 2. The number 1 is not considered prime.

product The answer of a multiplication problem.

proper fraction A fraction whose numerator is less than its denominator.

proportion An equation that states that two ratios are equal.

Pythagorean theorem In a right triangle, $a^2 + b^2 = c^2$, where a and b represent the legs and c represents the hypotenuse

quadrilateral A two-dimensional shape with four sides.

quotient The answer you get when you divide. *Example:* 10 divided by 5 is 2; the quotient is 2.

radius A line from the center of a circle to a point on the circle (half of the diameter)

ratio A comparison of two things using numbers.

reciprocal The multiplicative inverse of a fraction. For example, $\frac{2}{1}$ is the reciprocal of $\frac{1}{2}$.

rectangle   A parallelogram with four right angles.

remainder   The number left over after division. *Example:* 11 divided by 2 is 5, with a remainder of 1.

rhombus   A parallelogram with four equal sides.

right angle   An angle whose measure is 90 degrees.

scale drawings   A representation of an object that has been enlarged or reduced according to the proportions of its original size.

scalene triangle   A triangle with no equal sides.

scatter plots   A graph of plotted points that show the relationship between two sets of data.

simplify   To combine like terms and reduce an equation to its most basic form.

square   A parallelogram with four equal sides and four right angles.

squared units   Units of area formed by multiplying a unit of length by itself once.

square of a number   The product of a number and itself, such as 4^2, which is 4×4.

statistics   The study of collection, organization, and interpretation of mathematical data.

straight angle   An angle that measures 180 degrees.

subtraction   An arithmetic operation that takes away one value from another.

subtrahend   In subtraction, the number being subtracted.

sum   The sum of two numbers is the total of two numbers added together.

surface area   The sum of the area of the faces of a three-dimensional figure.

table   Graphic organizer that arranges information into columns and rows.

trends   In a graph, the change over time of a set of data.

triangle   A polygon with three sides.

variables   Letters used to stand in for numbers.

volume   A cubic measurement that measures how many cubic units it takes to fill a solid figure.

whole numbers   The counting number and zero.

width   The horizontal distance between two sides of an object.

NOTES

NOTES

NOTES

Special FREE Offer from LearningExpress

LearningExpress guarantees that you will be better prepared for, and score higher on, law enforcement exams.

Go to the LearningExpress Practice Center at www.LearningExpressFreeOffer.com, an interactive online resource exclusively for LearningExpress customers.

Now that you've purchased LearningExpress's *Math Skills for Law Enforcement Exams*, you have **FREE** access to:

- **An online practice test, designed to help you prepare for the math section of any law enforcement exam**
- **Immediate scoring** and **detailed answer explanations**
- A **customized diagnostic report** to benchmark your skills and focus your study

Follow the simple instructions on the scratch card in your copy of *Math Skills for Law Enforcement Exams*. Use your individualized access code found on the scratch card and go to www.LearningExpressFreeOffer.com to sign in. Start practicing online right away!

Once you've logged on, use the spaces below to write in your access code and newly created password for easy reference:

Access Code: _____   Password: _____